Anonymity

---

THE SECRET LIFE
OF AN
AMERICAN
FAMILY

·

SUSAN BERGMAN

WARNER BOOKS

A Time Warner Company

The author gratefully acknowledges permission to reprint material from the following previously published sources: Excerpt from " The Other Side of the River" from *The World of the Ten Thousand Things* by Charles Wright. Copyright © 1990 by Charles Wright. Reprinted by permission of Farrar, Straus & Giroux, Inc., Notes from the Underground *by Fyodor Dostoyevsky, translated by Jessie Coulson (Penguin Classics, 1972), copyright © Jessie Coulson, 1972, reproduced by permission of Penguin Books Ltd;* Collected Poems of Elinor Wylie, *copyright © 1929 by Alfred A. Knopf, Inc., copyright renewed 1957 by Edwina S. Rubenstein. Reprinted by permission of Alfred A. Knopf, Inc.; excerpt from Perpetua of Africa in* The Acts of Christian Martyrs, *translated by Herbert Musurillo, 1972. Reprinted by permission of Oxford University Press; lyrics from "Can't Help Lovin' Dat Man," written by Jerome Kern and Oscar Hammerstein II, copyright © 1927 Polygram International Publishing, Inc. Copyright renewed. Used by permission. All rights reserved; excerpt from* Soap Opera Digest, *Febrary 5, 1991, issue. Used by permission.*

Brief quotations appearing in the text are from the following sources: page 11, Lord Byron, "When We Two Parted"; page 13, Richard Howard, "With the Remover to Remove," The Comedy of Art; *page 13, Paul Monette,* Borrowed Time: An AIDS Memoir; *page 26, John Berryman, "Dream Song 145,"* The Dream Songs; *page 169, Electra, Richard Strauss, libretto by Hugo von Hofmannsthal; page 188, Emily Dickinson, no. 203,* Final Harvest; *page 188, George T. Wright,* The Poet in the Poem; *page 193, Richard Howard; page 193, Jorie Graham, "Orpheus and Eurydice,"* The End of Beauty; *page 193, Louise Glück, "Marathon,"* The Triumph of Achilles.

This Warner Books edition is published by arrangement with Farrar, Straus and Giroux, 19 Union Square West, New York, NY 10003

Warner Books, Inc., 1271 Avenue of the Americas, New York, NY 10020

Ⓦ A Time Warner Company

Printed in the United States of America
First Trade Printing: August 1995
10 9 8 7 6 5 4 3 2 1

Library of Congress Cataloging-in-Publication Data

Anonymity / Susan Bergman
    p. cm
Originally published : Farrar, Straus and Giroux, 1994.
ISBN 0-446-67119-3
1. Heche, Don, 1938-1983—Health 2. Bergman, Susan. 3. AIDS
(Disease)—Patients—United States—Biography. 4. AIDS (Disease)—Patients—
Family relationships. 5. Gay fathers—United States—Biography. I. Title.
RC607.A26H383   1995
362. 1' 969792 0092—dc20
[b]   95-8996
                                                       CIP

Through the dispersing vertigo of trance
I fixed my eyes upon your countenance,
Which is, to me, the elemental stuff
of beauty perfected, and the mask put off . . .

—ELINOR WYLIE

It's linkage I'm talking about,
*   and harmonies and structures*
And all the various things that lock our wrists to the past.

Something infinite behind everything appears,
*   and then disappears.*
It's all a matter of how
*   you narrow the surfaces.*
It's a matter of how you fit in the sky.

> *from:* "The Other Side of the River"
> Charles Wright

With deepest gratitude for the constellation of lives which illumine and grace mine:

Nancy, Abigail, and Anne Heche are champions and I love them. Their consistent willingness to read and check facts and care for me and each other made the story told in *Anonymity* truer.

Susan Prickett gave me her name and her craft, and the sense that the women in our family are strong.

Anthony Walton formulated the plan of action and saw it through in ways I'm just beginning to know. He is a splendid thinker, friend, and writer, and the finest of generals.

Robley Wilson is the first editor to give my essays a place in the *North American Review*. His early and open-handed championing of my writing will forever go unmatched.

DeWitt Henry, Daniel Halpern, and Bill Henderson I want to thank for their careers of support and meticulous reading which they have devoted to writers in their fine journals *Ploughshares, Antaeus*, and in the *Pushcart Prize* volumes. I'm honored.

The compassion and skill of several people helped shape this book and my life as I wrote. I want to thank: Barton and Beth Bergman, Jeff Thompson, Calvin Bedient, Carolyn Forche, Tobias Wolff, Tim Lowly, Mark Rudman, Philip Yancey, Alison Dalton, Victoria Smith, Paul Breslin, Phyllida Burlingame, and for his indispensable wisdom, Jonathan Galassi.

I want to express appreciation also to those whose insightful reading was for me an unalloyed pleasure: Amanda Urban, Ron Hansen, Michael Dorris, Steve Martin, Helen Vendler, Nan Kaehler, Susan Crown, Gail Kienit, Flori McMillen, Marie Hayes, Geoff and Genie Shields, Al Copland, Robert and Nancy Kuppenheimer, and Herb and Roberta Nechin; and to Dorothy Doumakes and the Ragdale Foundation for the sustenance of space in which to write.

My children Elliot, Elise, Natalie, and Bennet are beings of their own order, whose lives will most bear the unforeseen costs and, with hope, the lasting benefits of living in mercy instead of shame. These children unlock my wrists to the future.

*I*t was not until my father died that we found out about his other life. Then our other lives began. The last time I saw him was an early Sunday morning in March 1983. I drove downtown from Yonkers, where I was living, to visit him at Bellevue Hospital. The orange winter sun threaded the eye of the bridge and the blue veins of the East River. He turned from the window at the sound of my footsteps in the hall, his head floating above his shoulders, which balanced precariously like the cross bar of a capital T on his listing stalk of a body. I didn't want him to take a step for fear the rays of sunlight, the distant wake of a barge on the river, the draft from my breathing, would topple him. The doctor had called to tell me he'd fallen and hit his head. These were the last stages of dementia. He was forty-five years old.

From his stained eyes he evidenced no recognition at first—he would like some water, please. "Nurse, I need water before the Union Guard . . . they are almost . . . if you could help me." He was going to fall over again. I lunged toward the window to prop him up. "Sweetie?" he said, puzzled and weeping now. "Sweetie?" The sudden hilarity of a visitor overtook him. He straightened his hair, which had slipped back, widening his forehead. He smoothed his beard. "I didn't think you'd come."

To hold them side by side: the image of the stranger dying in the faded blue hospital gown and the familiar image of the church music director calling his four children up from the front pew to sing—how to make them fit. His expansive, bright-faced charm and his yellow, lifeless skin. What he professed and how he must have lived.

We knew so little about his disease that early. The suppurating patches of skin, the heaving cough, disoriented wandering, narrowing vision, recurring fevers and chills, the tease of the cycle—one day up, the next abed. What seemed incalculable and unique for him was in fact part of an increasingly knowable pattern visible to those who had been alerted or had lived through it with a lover once or twice before recognizing the plague taking hold in themselves. We were not privy to the pattern. The experimental treatments he underwent seemed to us like last-ditch efforts to subdue his fresh-named symptoms.

Even now I must review the evidence—clues traced to a source: the imported candy in his drawer; his toupee and tanning gel and poppers; recurring hepatitis; the "roommates" he stayed with when he was released from the hospital; Grand Central Station, where I saw him waiting once outside the men's room before he noticed me. I am one of his daughters. A sleuth, a dependent.

And now I am a tourist of my father's secrets. What unimagined appeal must his life away from us have offered, so compelling as to cost him all he had? What strain must he have felt, what edgy caution—discretion, he would have called it—kept just enough distance between one appearance and another? How alone he must have been. Daddy, I want to see behind your face, one face, one brokenness, and then hold the reworked memories dear. Because I loved him, and wasn't always able to show it, and because to recover the person he'd disguised is to unearth for the first time our own lives' buried artifacts.

If the family is where we first learn about ourselves and others, it is also often the cradle of misidentity and isolation. Our false fronts, the insincere roles we adopt to survive, the ways the "victims" of loss endure and recover, combined with our interpretations (affecting both the images that appear to us and how we ourselves are perceived), the early influences that give shape to sexuality—these are the shards that each of us sorts and reassembles and, finally, must pour our lives from.

And so the stories my sisters and mother and I began to tell each other a few years ago, our accounts of more recent retrievals, start with the familiar facts of childhood and are retold over time, as if from the inside—stripped of their outer slippery husk. We say who we are because of and in spite of my father, at once thankful and struck with dread. He had so much to protect. We have all this to unearth.

In the stories I tell here I have not softened the edges

or revised our initial shock. If I sucked too long on the bones of my mother's and sisters' and my own hurts, I have since been attuned to others' severer agonies. What choices haven't been paid for double or triple in a death from AIDS?

ANONYMITY

Turandot: Gli enigmi sono tre, la morte una!
Caleph: No, no! Gli enigmi sono tre, una la vita!
—PUCCINI

(There are three riddles, but one death!
No, no! There are three riddles, and one life!)

1   /   The summer of 1977, after my
sophomore year in college, I took a job lifeguarding at a
hotel rooftop swimming pool eight stories above the boardwalk in Atlantic City. It was the summer gambling muscled
in, and the sleepy ghetto town was intoxicated with the crisp
new bills casino lords waved under every soon to be displaced nose. In July, the Marlborough-Blenheim Hotel still
lent the ramshackle grandeur of its lobby to deals deals
deals, regardless of the wrecking ball that barely one year
later would polish off what explosives hadn't collapsed. Or-
ganized crime's entourage, which the white-haired ladies
stood up in town meetings to decry, had assembled. What
I hadn't seen before that summer in the way of off-center

sex and other permutations of greed, I learned breathing
salt air in the company of transients and gamblers and those
who serviced them.

Joe tended poolside bar on weekends as the mostly
foreign tourists drank blender mix-ups that made them sink
when I tried to teach them to swim. "Mickey Finns." Joe
scraped his voice into my ear with a laugh. "It'll put 'em
on the bottom every time." On steamy afternoons before
the blackjack tables' first cards had been dealt, to the carnival rantings of the penny arcade below, I stayed sober on
the virgin mint nostalgia coolers Joe concocted in honor of
the Ferris wheel or the green-and-white-striped trolley or
the faded beach umbrellas. "Here's to you, Sappho" (he
kept an eye on me), "to saving lives. Do it while there's still
time!"

Joe first started calling me Sappho on one of the few
rainy Saturdays that summer. He pulled it like a paisley
handkerchief from his hat, or out of the overcast air, I
guessed. At the time the name stood for the whole secret
world to which he alluded and belonged, Mafia dandies,
union men, the multiracial women who came and went for
free drinks and a couple of laughs. I held my image of his
image of me like a pose hardly apropos for an out-of-her-
element Ohio girl taking in, for the first time, an Atlantic
seaboard town. Sappho was a woman in a black bathing
suit that buttoned down the front.

By the time Joe finished his crossword puzzle, the laundry crew had sent up the day's hot-from-the-dryer towels
which were my living: a dollar tip per towel draped over
the gentleman's arm, a two-dollar tip for showing the lady
to her chaise. There were the man and woman who pulled
up a chair for me between them and spoke in slurred voices

about many-partnered sex. How it worked, how it would feel. My experiments in the direction of physical intimacy had been modeled on Western Literary Romance as commonly available in the *Poetry of Love Anthology*, historical novels, or the comic books in my grandparents' backwater grocery store which as a child I snuck under my skirt to read in the garage. One male and one female; a gradual crescendo in the same covered-wagon train; glances, "Shall I compare thee to a summer's day?"; a mountain pass; a soda shop; the top down, taken by storm; "There be none of Beauty's daughters/ With a magic like thee"; marriage. With nothing in my life up to that point to help translate what the couple was asking me to do, I can't remember much of what they described, except that as I got up to go, the gray-skinned man rolled his head on his shoulder and said, "Think about it, Pussy-Pussy?" Despite my arms' length refusal, I had participated, listening, my awkwardness a hitch of conscience even as the wife began to coax, my fear the green trapeze I swung on over their heads. They seemed lonely to me, so I went with them for a lobster dinner after work and rode my bicycle home down the boardwalk.

There was the flawless, smooth-skinned girl exactly my age, whom Joe said Mr. Koroner kept, and whose red toenails he would rub as he walked by her chair. She simply sat, without a book, in the sun, never going near the water. If the general questions I posed could be met with one-word answers, she would say yes or no; if not, she looked at the door, or petted the subtle incline under her ribs with her long, spread fingers until I went away. Some days it was just the two of us for hours. I wanted to know where she'd found her scanty armor, and the way it worked.

The queens who snuck in in pods of three despised me for my breasts. They giggled in vigorous falsettos and spat directly at my feet, rubbing themselves against the pool lights or the wooden slats of the chairs or the deck rails. Masquerading as girls, they played out their episodes of how girls must behave, calling a hair out of place déshabillé, trading an orange bracelet for a purple fringed scarf. My thighs were not right, the way they didn't rub together at the top like theirs. I could see why they preferred men. They leaned way out over the boardwalk, all calling at once. They primped and rehearsed, the artifice of gendered accoutrement cubed. At first they came to swim and chide, but as the summer wore on and the crowds thinned, so did their act. My part in their carnival was cut to stagehand, towel bearer. They had gotten to me and found the target wanting.

For the photographer who milled around the sun deck in plaid trunks with cameras hanging off his back I was a sunny prop. In the back of my disorderly cupboards I still find the inch-square blue plastic key-chain peek portraits of the French-Canadian duo with their arms around Sappho, smiling; the Hollywood mogul with his black bikini and me; Ed, the other lifeguard who loved the racetrack, and me. It was part of the resort appeal of souvenirs and sideshows that went with the job. And there were two identical-twin would-be gynecologist pool managers, whom we could not tell apart and who liked it that way. They were my boss and would jump in the water after me when I was swimming and try to pull me under. I slicked on suntan lotion before diving in, and one or the other of them would wrestle the great oily half-fish Sappho till she nearly drowned.

The hotel manager who gave me the job was what I

then called a bachelor friend of my father's. Fortyish, masterfully handsome, he was rumored to have fathered the child the owner's wife was about to have. But the owner wasn't worried. "It's his own rumor," Joe confided to me. "The fellow likes it behind closed doors."

"Queen" was the "bachelor's" term for men who frolicked in the open. He owed my father a favor was how I heard it, so my friend got a job in the office answering phones for the summer and I got to work at the pool. I heard my father arguing with the manager past midnight sometimes on the telephone. He would wrap and unwrap himself in the rubber cord. That summer I knew nothing of being kept, or of my father and his friends, or of the other Sappho, but I liked that name better than my old one. Joe made it sound learned and notorious, and when he introduced me, no one mixed me up with anyone else.

August in Ohio emptied out horses and baseball, marigold gardens and salamander streams. We toted books and coins to the tree house and traded stories for silver dollars. I'd turned twelve in May. If a boy loved me, he could hold me out over the edge of the wood-plank platform in the air for an hour without letting go. If a boy loved you, he would tie your wrists to a high branch with a thousand knots.

I didn't sign my first poems. They fit on 3-by-5 cards the exact size of what I thought and felt, which was the perfect size to report on Hopi Indians, or the Declaration of Independence, or nightingales and their nests. No name. That way Jackie, the neighbor's German cousin visiting for the summer, would be overcome with a pure, undesignated passion when he discovered them rolled up and tied with ribbons, tucked under his pillow or in his shoes.

The beloved turns the handwritten page over to look for a name, any name. Who could have sent me this? It means what I mean. I will never have to speak again. It is what my life has meant all along to discover. Finding no name, he turns back to the words which burn behind his eyes, it is the words of the one whom he has loved forever— THE WORDS. *I will go to her; she is here with me. She will take us in our arms.*

I pictured that if I left off my name, the words would loosen from me and the page so they could float out toward a cosmic, amorphous love-at-large that would somehow settle on Jackie as he slept. Isn't that what potions do? I would happen along, the poem's remedies cast over him. He would declare his mutual absorption in the nameless vocabulary of hearts and moons. We would wander in the fields and woods, or sit on the roof of the house being built down the road. He would hold out his hand in a fist in front of me and ask me to pull up on his thumb, which he liked me to do so he could fart. Then he would kiss me. He was confident and courageous enough to do such things even in front of parents. He was seventeen. He had an accent.

The summer before that, my great-grandmother had died and left me all her books. My family had driven to her house in Indiana and told me that I could take as many as would fit into one cardboard box, which I filled and emptied and rearranged until I could fit all of James Whitcomb Riley Hoosier Poet, Byron, Keats, and Shelley, some sheet music with Art Nouveau ladies in flowing dresses, a few bound copies of an early women's magazine, and her notebooks and genealogies. Her dying started me thinking about death and poems. So I promptly requested baptism into my parents' separatist Baptist church of sixteen or so parishioners—to give up my life and replace it with the Word, to die as the pastor laid me back in the water, and to resurrect. And I began to transform lines from Byron's poems into facsimiles of my own, layering grace over ardor.

As though no one would notice—who had ever read George Gordon, Lord Byron, but my great-grandmother? —I borrowed liberally. Revision meant a shift of focus from a description of the beloved to being the beloved. I was now the thee of the lines, I the beauty, the one waiting, the betrayer, no credit to the original. There were places I could go in the poems where I could not trespass in the everyday. Things to be. I was in the air of the poems, I the articulating will that compelled the circle of desire to turn around me, and to return. There were ladders and hallways, chandeliers, forbidden keys, long golden hair, a wand, a mountain I moved or moved through. I would read Byron's poems, then open to the front of the volume and carefully lift the yellowed tissue back from the poet's portrait etched on the flyleaf, for inspiration. He was my first and last muse (a concept I have since understood to be a corruption of the female-as-inspiration). But he worked for me. Every other line rhymed without fail or slant.

In Ohio, no one noticed that the poems were Byron-writ-adolescent. But the pastor who had baptized me, the uncle of my love, either found one of the poems in its hiding place and demanded to have the complete work or, as I suspect happened, was presented with the series, ribbons and all, as a great, hilarious betrayal of me by the villain Jackie. He knew. The poems would be burned ceremonially in the incinerator the two families shared. How did he know? Our lives leave clues. Passion and words are neither pure nor unattached. They are profoundly fastened to their sources. Their spells wear off. You wake up to find you have adored an ass.

A sort of tribunal of spiritual discipline took place that evening, structured as the trial of Hester Prynne. I remember the "logical conclusions," prostitution and fornication, since they sounded alike. My mother left the room. My father spoke to me in a rushed voice about how inappropriate such lustful poems were coming from a member of the Bride of Christ. I was part of them, he said, an ambassador, the old man of me put away, the new man wearing a white wedding dress. I don't say this to mock him now, and less to mock my own sincere participation in the outward acts of my faith. He was both terrified and compelled by my imagination, and his own, which could have its roots, he feared, only in the wicked practices of the pagan world from which he had withdrawn. His strategy for righteousness was separatism: we would run from temptation, not write it down. I'm not sure which was worse in his mind, the poems or the illustrations.

What more graphic way for a child to learn the attachment of words to their sources than for her own—borrowed as they were from a passionate poet—to be read aloud in front of a roomful of people so as to convict her and horrify them. You write the words: you will carry their praise or blame. These things didn't really happen, I told them. This isn't me, it's someone else. But, to my interrogators, words equaled acts; concepts (in the hands of the unsympathetic), crime. I am still torn, actual Reader, between wanting to address you sincerely (if it were possible), without the interference of artifice, and wanting the art to show between the two of us. As I listened to my transgression, it sounded rhythmic and eloquent, and though they stumbled over the loopy cursive, someone in the poems spoke exactly what I meant.

It had failed to work in a mighty way, the anonymity: the words claimed me whether or not I called them by my name. Not only the words but their intent. I stopped crying when I slept. They taught me well, whatever else they meant for me to learn, that to begin to write something down is to admit the secret, which will always give you away.

My books were forbidden, as was writing poems. For a rare, indecisive moment, my parents and the pastor (who to this day hectors a dwindling band of the adamant) discussed whether I should submit to the discipline of excommunication or receive a spanking. How old is a twelve-year-old girl? The pastor sat me on his lap and recited parts of verses I wish I could remember: the pure of heart, the good the better the best, think on these things, no doubt. He said I would be watched, vigilance, penitence, abstinence. Didn't I like to play with girls my age? Couldn't I learn to sew? I was not allowed to say goodbye to Jackie, whose eighteenth birthday I also missed. I had wanted it to go: "When we two parted / In silence and tears, / Half brokenhearted / To sever for years, / Pale grew thy cheek and cold, / Colder thy kiss; / Truly that hour foretold / Sorrow to this."

On the thrust stage of the Guthrie Theatre, in slow motion as the houselights dim, a mass of figures in the heat of an Algerian midday advance and recede to the accompaniment of the Electric Arab Orchestra's whiny short-winded repetitions. Philip Glass has written the music for Jean Genet's *The Screens*. The drumbeat and the human commotion reduce to the twitch of a shoulder here, the face's tic against flies, a slow hand rises to sweep the forehead there. A shudder, a spasm, the bodies feel perpetual and chronic.

The whole momentum of the six-hour event—ninety characters, the golden skirts of the whore (dinner break of beef with currant and pine nuts, tabouli, eggplant salad), red flames in the orange grove, red umbrellas of the mourners—flushes toward oblivion. "I worked so hard to erase myself," Said, the central character says to his wife, Leila, who is so ugly he keeps her in a full body veil. And in the end, as Genet tells the story, this is what his character achieves, not a better life or an afterlife, but nothing.

The play's last three scenes take place overhead in the land of the dead. Heavy netting strung between the ceiling and the audience groans with the weight of its ever-replenished cache. The newly deceased crash one after the other through the paper portals and exclaim, "Oh, this is not what I'd expected!" After the third or fourth time the audience mouths the words with the actors. Said is not well after years in prison, years as society's kicking boy. They expect him any moment now, the dead, who roll, clumped in the net in their white robes like wetted cotton wads, humming. But Said makes it, somehow, outside the realm of people in the net. He escapes both life and afterlife: that one alleviation Genet could conceive for the self from the vantage of his life as orphan, thief, inmate, prostitute, writer. "Said is like me," Leila says, "he wants everything to fuck up as fast as it can."

So did my father, who was almost as clever as Genet with aesthetic consolations. Refusing to distinguish between the stage and himself, the oblivion he enacted played in the cramped theater of his body to harsh consequence.

He died one stranger at a time until he finally caught it and could pass it along.

"O you must have a Bluebeard closet!" says Richard Howard, who early on abandoned his. "Everybody does." His poems sanction in passage after passage what I imagine my father would have liked not to hide. The dead's secrets are tough to force. A private room in an indigent ward, the name of an Episcopal minister to gay men, phone calls charged to my account that I can trace. I go back over the veiled signals: "Family man," he kept insisting, "family man—I adore my perfect, model, churchgoing wife—and what a family man resists makes him a square in the round world. You know this new scene of mine, Andy Warhol, von Furstenberg; people whisk me around town in their limousines. Clients of mine. I was supposed to meet them at this bar where the most gorgeous tall black-haired woman can't take her eyes off me. She leads me toward the backstairs and I tell her, Family man happily married, four beautiful children. Upstairs she's a man. Freak of nature! The entire floor is pulsing with small colonies of partners in the dark. Men more beautiful than the next, with muscles and fiery loins. The pattern breaks—no, more fluid—it absorbs color and momentum, stalk in, stalk out, breath of a single beast, heave, stroke, as if it would dissolve me inside its scales. *Everyone's getting exactly what he wants.* I didn't belong there, sweetheart, and knew it as soon as . . . Clients take me there. You would like them. They wouldn't believe I have a daughter your age. Their barbers come to their apartments to shave them."

This is the part of the story he told me, his confidante: Better not mention this to your mother. What he told my sister when she walked in on him in the bathroom fumbling with her mascara was that from so far away—a poorly lit room, the raised piano top casting a steep shadow—it would be hard for people to see who he was.

What kept my father's existence secret was less the lack of evidence, I suppose, than his meticulous track-covering and refutation. And, no doubt, there was some confusion on his part—was he himself a well-wrought mask? Blue-beard, your family is right here with you. We are the part of the persona most put on and taken off. It is getting stuffy in here. The more I write about him, the more I feel like Noah's son who, finding his father drunk and without clothes, held back the flaps of his tent and laughed. I'm not uncovering my father's nakedness, I'm getting some air.

Until *The New York Times* ran an extensive article on it on February 6, 1983, few outside the homosexual under-ground knew much about AIDS. The small-print names of my father's miscellany of diseases I'd been hearing from the Bellevue doctors were euphemisms that couldn't begin to describe the horror. Cancer, we told our friends, a mild case of skin cancer and pneumonia. According to the early press reports, the first cases took hold in the most promis-cuous. Estimates of 1,100 partners average, per death. Within a year of their report, 75 percent of the cases studied died. To New York and back on business, to San Francisco, his ship coming in, could I lend him airfare, he would stay with friends. Could I just read him the numbers on my credit card over the phone, please sorry, he got there but he couldn't get back.

So much suddenly made sense: his hepatitis, rectal surgeries, the case of crabs he pretended our mother had contracted from someone else. She sat at the kitchen table telling us about our father picking out the lice from her pubic hair and blaming her. "Did you borrow someone else's bathing suit?" Not only the itch and burn, but the deceit again, always deflecting the blame elsewhere, onto us.

I walked up to the roof of our building in Yonkers and watched a tugboat on the Hudson haul a rusty barge under the George Washington Bridge. Back downstairs I read the article again. He wasn't Haitian. He didn't use drugs. Maybe he used drugs; I'd look for needle marks. I read it again. No one stands on a rug that cannot be pulled out from under her: I was the daughter of a cocksucker.

"Just nod," I would say to them at the hospital. "I'm not asking for a sentence, just a confirmation."

"You'll have to talk with your father."

"In his delirium my father thinks I'm the Union Guard. He hardly breathes. Doctor, you would think he would want someone he loves to know something about him."

"The prognostic groups he falls into are not good. Anything we know is so inconclusive at this point that . . ."

"Anything we ever know, fine. Of course it's AIDS, or you would tell me." The cold March sun sliced along the bridge cables strung over the East River. Tubes and incisions. The bridge laced all the way over, its neat stitches tiresome. If not for the random colors of cars outside his window, each with its passengers trying to talk, if not for the low boats, fly at the window.

"You nurses are so lazy," my father said from his bed, mistaking me. "I will not let you destroy my life." Along the hospital parking lot they'd planted acanthus trees that stank like the necks of sweaty children. The smell wiped out the disinfectant and his blue gown tied once in the back.

They called me one day that week, sorry, wondering if I would release the body to science. There were three dimes, some small tins of hard imported candy, and a jar of bronzing cream in his bedside table drawer. I said no, we would ship the body whole to his mother and sister. They could dress him up.

Your father dies: you wish you didn't think, Good riddance. Every curse falls flat. What are we celebrating, celebrities? How many patches for the quilt now, O ye who stitch in sympathy? Drag out Tennyson and his long-winded moan for his young friend; flash back to Patroclus. How black is the day of pictures to the gallery wall? I have been waiting to say this. My sisters and I are calmer now. My mother has a job and calls us. We are calm. We watch it on television, the parade of Victims. We are calm. We are not men.

The men have written poems and empathetic screenplays for each other, having undergone society's inflictions. Their versions master the neat shift from rage to tenderness, loose ends to closure: they make lousy art out of their losses, hurrying, before the subject is passé—not another AIDS drama! I'm waving my arms now. Courage, dignity, a forced bloom of humor, elevation of his suffering. National Public Radio chronicles the lover's last days. I hurry out to buy the last dress Perry Ellis designed. The men are dying. The men are loosing torrents of rage at the government, the Centers for Disease Control, fury with eruptive force so it doesn't wash back on them—yelling at their lungs' most muscular pitch. Best blamers. How is this my fault? Yet I'm not allowed—my own heart forbids it—to yell back. There are others too, I whisper. I want to pipe down. They will need whatever strength we all have. But don't look to me, yet.

After seven years the dreams have stopped. I dug my fingers into his eye sockets and pulled with my thumbs under his chin to try to tear the mask away. He came into my house and rearranged the furniture, pasting layers of grass cloth on the walls. No one else in the dream recognized him. When I screamed, he flinched and blinked, sometimes cowering behind the couch. My father played keyboard instruments, mostly church organs and dinner-club grands. He had five children; I will introduce you to them, two dead, who did what he said.

The homosexual father prays before dinner and compares his calamity to Job's. The homosexual father sits in group therapy with his confused children and unsuspecting wife and discusses phantom trouble. The homosexual father is so frightened of his daughter's ordinary development that he finds a way to torment her for menstruating. The homosexual father contracts hepatitis and insists it was the seafood he ate, which the rest of his family had too. He is sick and yellow when his children meet the bill collectors at the door. The homosexual father disapproves as his daughters flirt with older men. The homosexual father lives as though his were the only life.

That life—a lack, gaping, insatiable, cast out onto the waters—will come back to your children, whom I intend to tell. I will say, You do not belong to the family you believe you belong to. It is not your fault for thinking the collar and tie before your eyes, the toupee, the poppers he does before he has sex with your mother (just to survive what his father did to him) are safe. How he seems . . . Beware. It's not your fault.

The year before he died—the days he felt "back to normal"—I would run into him on the street and we would have lunch that I would pay for, all right. He would taste his food, lick his fingers, and then tear off a piece of meat or cheese, which he would put in my baby's mouth. Go to HELL, DADDY. Go to hell every single fucking jack he ever fucked or was fucked by, the zillion Grand Central Station royalty men's-room flight attendant Times Square suicides. I don't mean it. I mean it, but I could never say it to your face.

I was holding the baby. You said, "I don't think I want him to call me Granddad, please. Teach him to call me, oh, I don't know, Skipper."

We would walk back to the large formal apartment where my father was staying and chat with the man who kept him during the months after the family was locked out of the Ocean City beach house for not paying the rent. The man talked about his ministry to the gay community. He was trying to let me in on my father's condition. He felt around conversationally to see if he could pass along the burden of my father's care. My father was proud of the enormous room and pointed to the oil portraits, stumbling over the names. He looked to the minister for correction. His skin was "rowdy," pea, onion-peel yellow—it was my father's skin; I cannot get it right. His tongue, as he tried to moisten his lips, was white with fungus. "Take some grapes with you," he offered, "for the ride home."

2 / *T*o listen to us talk, mostly on the phone these days, is to overhear our healing. Last night Anne called. She had been drawing after a long day on the set, free-drawing with her new pencils. She wanted to try a child's head from memory, so began with a rounded shape, keeping the pencil going. To draw a child might uncover what remained in her of her growing up before the deaths, which were the wall she was trying to see through. First our father; then, three months later, our eighteen-year-old brother—it was the early morning, still dark—had driven his car into a tree. A round, soft head appeared before her on the page, but as she drew, the child developed heavy eyebrows and wrinkles around the mouth. It was wearing

eye makeup and the nose was sharper than a child's. He had too much hair.

"The face grew as ugly as . . . It looked like the face in that painting you did of the woman who was really a man," she said. Across the top of the page she wrote *Man Wearing a Wig*. "As soon as I wrote that, I knew I was drawing Dad. I got the shoulders done fast and went down the trunk to his groin. His arms pressed flat against his sides. There was his penis; I said, What am I doing? This is awful, then his hands covered himself."

It was him, all right. It helps to say it out loud to each other. Not only him, but ourselves, the parts we can identify. "It's the tension I store in my neck and chin that I'm trying to let go," Anne says; "touch me there and I bruise." One day we will be well enough, we'll have become generous toward him.

I cannot tell whether in my memories of my younger sisters they are laughing as they hitch their long dresses up to run, or if they are only calling back and forth. They knew each other's secrets, and seemed blessed, too, by having an older brother we were all to lose to an early death. From the distance ten and twelve years' difference in age makes I must have looked gigantic and solitary, intent at the piano, gawky as I strode between the woods and hand-hoed garden the colors of my water paints. The river I imagined separating us seemed always too swift to ford—on one bank my adolescence, on the other their first words. My studies away from home deepened the breach. They shared a bedroom, and on holidays and at my wedding they dressed alike. I was their half-mother, calling them "the children." They refused to keep their toys in place. I waited for them—eager and anxious in the lobby of the hospital—to be born.

By the time our father died and, so soon after, Nathan, besides Christmas and high-school graduations, the deaths were the only events we knew each other by. Suddenly, with a single grief, we were three grown daughters whose mother wept for days in the small upstairs apartment she had rented near the ocean. The youngest daughter walked out to the water's edge and watched. The middle daughter went off in the bartender's arms to gifts of gold chains and diamonds. I arrived the day after the crash and told the preacher what passage, what hymn, what heaven.

Abigail, the middle one, claimed the body. She collected Nathan's billfold at the police station before she went down to the morgue with her boyfriend and looked right at the face, swollen from the broken neck. She let what she could register. He looked older, as though he were calmly resting. The light had seeped from his skin. Nathan and Abi were headed for college in a few weeks. They would take turns driving. She turned and said, "We need to pick up Susan at the airport." I was coming from Chicago, alone. When I first saw her at the gate, she was the dead one who spoke; then she was alive in my arms, or I was in her arms, trembling, and she was saying nothing again but was holding on to me as tightly as she ever had. She had seen him last, both alive and dead, was just a year younger than he was. Her hair smelled salty.

The funeral was more sideshow than solemn. When a graduating senior, actor, cutup, darling dies, the high-school choir sings "Love Lift Us Up Where We Belong" and wearing two-toned robes, sobs about the world below.

Everyone has a memory and a chance to stand up front at the microphone to share it. Death is a public opportunity. I was there when . . . I remember . . . He is standing on his hands in heaven; no doubt, he has the angels wearing punk-rock ties. A quick death: he was gone before he knew what was happening. "You all knew Nathan," says Miss Ocean City, whom he loved, pausing to swallow, "in the high-school corridors, on the tennis courts; you knew him for his spunk, courage, faith." Spared a future, saved time. Well-meaning, the village lines up outside the church. At the morning vigil reporters check their facts.

The daughters sit beside their mother in the front row with their heads down. Three months earlier our father had been buried, and the shock of his disease exposed to the family, who quickly covered his tracks. If that's what he was, what was wrong with us? It was 1983 in New York; his set of symptoms had just been given a name. When I look up, I feel myself being watched. I am conscious of my expression and resent my awareness of an audience, as though Nathan losing the curve on Steelmantown Road were not concern enough. They are more sorry for us than they are for him. They barely knew him. I want to hoard the hurt. This was our brother, our mother's son. The display of grief is an unbearable distraction from the grief.

We try to stay together. Here is your sting, Death. One year, the year is gone. Two years pass, and the gatherings are stiffer. Three years (shouldn't we find something else to talk about?), one resurrects in her behavior the lost child, one the self-destroying father, one the need to rescue and be rescued. Our roles tangle. We destroy one another's fragile equilibrium. Together, in one place the great hand reached down and plucked first one, then another. Now we play into the hand, dare the hand.

Anne speeds: God wouldn't dream of it, she says. Abigail bears whatever she can in her body. Death gets in you, but you retch it out, she tells us. You swallow death, its cabbage flavor and powdery dregs. If death isn't ready, it can crawl down your throat, but it will not digest. I keep eating and eating—I would quit if I could—and purging. You can beg me to stop all you want. Please, convince me. By now the urge is involuntary, her throat worn raw.

We look at each other six ways, our staring back and forth makes a braid. Mom carries apples and cheese between rooms, her heart's ease our presence under one roof, whatever the cost. My children climb up into the chair with me. The big hand appears out of the sky in my front window, and I flinch. I draw back, trying to surround the children —the hand is coming for me next. But when I look again, I think it means to soothe me; it has changed positions, though it is so huge it would scare even the mighty.

There is too much sorrow to remind each other of, too much unexplainable judgment. We agree at our mother's prompting to spend a week as a family on Nantucket, each from her own world with her own props, our remaining men, our grandmother, my children. Anne calls from the studio in New York after the rest of us have claimed bedrooms and unpacked. She has just started a job playing twins on a daytime soap, and in today's episode she lounged in a bubble bath talking on the phone. "My character is a sexpot," she moans, disappointed. "Sleazy?" Abi asks. "Strapless dresses with rhinestones, gambling debts, no doubt amnesia." The other twin, the writers tell her, is the good sister, but we aren't supposed to know this yet. Hush, hush, we put our fingers to our lips. "Break a leg?" the florist had suggested. "Write, Bubble, bubble, toil and trouble," we decided. Alstroemeria and African daisies, and a lavender-colored long-stemmed something, and fern.

We've never had a sister on TV. We want to lend her our dresses and favorite books. We want her to stay the same even with limousine rides to and from the studio, and "appearances"—or improve. Above all, we don't want to lose her, though we'll share. Anne will be theirs and ours, more public for a while, we guess. Our baby, their vamp. She's not going to be able to make it to Nantucket, after all, due to some union's impending strike. "Sorry it's not going to work out."

Abi and I tell her about our other awaited guest. Mother's widower friend from Boston is taking the ferry out tomorrow. From Mom's description he is handsome and slow. He calls it the three-year plan. "Fifty-two is none too soon," Abi is saying into the receiver. "What do they have to lose after both having had such long, happy marriages?" She smirks at Grandmother and me.

"They should have someone," says my grandmother, who has been a widow for many years and wishes a partner's care for her daughter. She is a reporter from the days of men and cigars only in the newsroom, admitted despite her gender because she delivered the whole story with a certain hard-bitten eloquence. Even now, refusing to wear her hearing aid, she reads our lips for the gist. "What did she say he was?" Grandmother stage-whispers. "He's still in love with the memory of his wife," Abi shouts, and to Anne, "See you later."

Mom and her guest drive into the village for lunch, and when I come in from the beach, I find Abi downstairs in Boston's bedroom, where he's stacked all his belongings neatly on the other single bed. "What are you doing in here, Miss Snoop?" I join her, keeping a lookout for the two of them. Mom has told Abi he brought some pictures of his former wife. She has them spread out on the dresser, and is studying the dark-haired stranger, careful not to get them out of order. Cancer shades the woman's expression: her smile seems not to pretend. "She looks like she could be his mother," Abi exaggerates. Grandmother has been looking for us and puts her finger to her lips as she hesitates in the doorway. She makes believe she's dusting our fingerprints off the photographs while peering over the top of her glasses. "My land, what an attractive woman," she hollers.

It's Father's Day. The evening fog mutes everything, all colors reduce to just a few grays and gray-greens. I trace the telephone wire almost to the second pole. Boston's daughter (whom we had invited to join us), hasn't shown up for dinner. As he pulls slowly into the driveway, Mom waves out the open car window like a homecoming queen. She bounds up the stairs, pushing her bangs back off her face. "Siasconcet is fabulous!" she cries. Boston sits down with me on the deck. Abi lets the door slam on her way out with lemonade and we watch the family of rabbits scatter. I mean to be kind but confess instead, While you were gone we talked about you, Boston. Abi flashes me a horrified look. He says we are most unfair, with a chuckle. This is the kind of man you can talk with if you read the daily papers—politically active, confident in his continued success. I bring up the subject of his lunch with George Will.

Mom is dressing for a cocktail party with his friends. He stands up and straightens the chairs before moving inside to shower.

"She hasn't told him about Dad yet," Abi says. He would not be plague-tolerant, I agree. The father-want wells up in both of us. I want the three daughters to have a father they never will, though we've auditioned several for the part. We imagine that man pulling a little girl who adores him in a wagon. Do you like girl children? Can you please *not* wear the look of having just woken up in our arms?

"Daddy—simply—isn't—coming—back," Anne announced a week ago. "Face it."

Also, we love him. No way to give him another chance, to try harder, to take it like a man. We sit on the deck and cry, about Boston's wife I think it is.

The cure for the father-want is to attempt to substitute other men. They play along for a while, attached to our devotion. If they don't work out, they can share our real father's blame. We want to tell the men how we grew up, in what country, what small farm down a long dirt road, how our family was religious to the point of martyrdom. Some want to hear, but most say, Would you like to have a drink, or, Would you like to read this manuscript of mine, or, right at first without the drink, "Come back to my room with me. I don't have to come down on you, we could just be there together." But I am not giving away, like perfume samples in department stores. And neither are we, and we want everyone to know this.

We have this being stared at in common, and we have this feeling of injury (though not quite of victimization) in common, and the wanting to tell each other, He did it again, that one, the one who, if we stood back to back, my bottom would rest on his—how far do you think we'd go—the one we wanted for a brother or a father. They send some form of flower-appeasement for their presumption, some way to make believe they were only complimenting us. We could use a free meal? Our father signal was not loud and clear, thank you? I'm sorry. We end up apologizing that they feel rejected. We explain our lives, adding in the true unhappiness lest they wait for a sudden gust of change. Not that they would wait. They aren't holding their breaths at all— it's a fix—the daughter spice, the flattery of how they will feel when their friends see us on TV, or in print, or on the avenue giving someone else directions, motioning around the corner to the place they want to go. They invite us, then forget. They ask the next daughters.

This is not an uncommon wish: to make love to the daughters one at a time. It is not uncommon that the daughters carry the wish inside them, turning it into obligation, making the wish cry or stand up on its hind legs by twisting it. We, too, make wishes. "I hope you know this is not my wish," they say, reaching toward our face.

The last time we met the wish, Anne and I were hunting for gold shoes. We had tried on the Kamali beaded jacket, the long one that came to the top of the thighs—Hopi Indian design—and the short bolero, black with primary-colored beads. We had put the hats on, the Patricia Underwood leather fedora best, and seen the black onyx teardrop earrings. We were trying not to have to make excuses for liking to do anything together that would give us a chance to laugh. I'm ahead of myself—we don't laugh yet. We can't even find one funny thing, which makes us doubly enraged at our father, who even if we understood him didn't have to take our brother, and at each other for still being so angry. "Every time I start getting close to a man physically, I cringe to think, Oh, now I'm feeling toward him the way Dad would have. That shuts me right down," Anne says. It's hard not to picture him humping the hair-weaver, the piano mike. We disgust ourselves.

Anne was holding the shoe she wanted the rude clerk to find the mate for, and as she handed the shoe to me to see what I thought, a piece of paper fell onto the floor. Neither of us noticed until the man bent over in front of us and held up the note, which said, *Hi, Anne, remember me?* Of course she did; they had met at a casting call a few years back and had kept in touch. He had taken a shower in her apartment the last time he was in New York from L.A. This time he needed a shower too, maybe, but I didn't think I knew him well enough to say. He is a painfully handsome young man, undecided on most issues, but full of passion, loose as a leather thong, with long dark hair that curls under his cap, which he took off so that Anne would recognize him before putting it back on.

"I know I'm a mess," he explained. "I've been follow-ing you two in and out of stores for an hour—how could you not notice me? I put the note in this shoe and you've carried it around the entire department." This in an in-credulous tone of voice about his spying and our obliv-iousness.

I offered my hand in introduction because Anne thought we knew each other. "Susan," I said. "Michael?"

"Oh, *you're* Susan. Boy, do you guys all look alike." Not if you look carefully. He'd been skiing in Austria with

Anne and Abigail. We've talked on the phone. I'd pictured him like this. He'd sent me stacks of scripts in the mail. He'd read my poems and called to talk.

So he attached himself to our shopping. We would take up too much of the sidewalk three astride so he would drop back a little, and Anne would try to finish her sentence, ". . . because after you and Abi moved out I was left to deal with Mom's emotions by myself. I'll come home when I'm ready." When I looked behind us, where Michael lagged a few paces back, he would shrug a little, or say something like "Hey, woman," knowing good and well that though all three of the daughters sometimes think of him, we were in the middle of a few hours we had stolen from our own lives to be together. He knew, but didn't care, and knew, too, that we wouldn't be able to come right out and ask him to go. We found the gold shoes at a place where Anne bought the cropped black boots I was wearing, in her size, and we hailed a cab to go across the park and pick up the dogs, but not before Michael, his wish in hand, presented it, and as I got into the car I thought I heard Anne answer, *Yes*, later, I'm talking with my sister; you see, my father burned at his own stake, my brother took the flaming arrows in his shoulder. But Michael did not hear any of this, of course, on the street corner with the rain slick on the curbs. And Anne and I had only a little time to decide about the jacket, which fit us both.

Because I am the oldest, or because I have more closets, because I am the only one of us who corresponds with my grandmother, and everyone comes here for holidays, I keep the family records, including photographs. We have more than most families must have, more posed and styled shots, head sheets for the children, who modeled or acted, and portraits of my father in hats, with a beard, with his teeth showing, with his lips closed. The pictures of Nathan make it even harder to remember him. There are several portraits of all of us together, which were kept in various talent agencies' files under "All-American Families," I suppose. Maybe someone would pay for the impression our family made. High concept: hawking how we put ourselves together, pasting our blond hair in place over our collage of smiles.

I stack the more recent pictures: oldest, middle, youngest—the three piles of proofs. We all do look so much like sisters because we are. It's about us now, though I wish I knew them better. I think about this and about how to move toward them when I barely know anything, not even the direction, except that the older we grow, the harder it must be to stay alive. Natural causes, accidentally driving fast, a gun loose as its oiled trigger, sex. Death drives us apart; it binds us together. These scissors feel light in my hands. The thought of them goes in as easily as the wheels left the curve of the road and crashed into a tree. We swim so far out alone from shore, alone the harder to see you, dear. Anne acts. Abigail binges.

After extremity, Isabella Leitner wrote her memoir of the death camp where she was taken with her family. She said:

If you are sisterless, you do not have the pressure, the absolute responsibility, to end the day alive. How many times did that responsibility keep us alive? I cannot tell. I can only say that many times when I was caught in a selection, I knew I had to get back

to my sisters, even when I was too tired to fight my way back . . .
Does staying alive not only for yourself, but also because someone
else expects you to, double the life force? Perhaps. Perhaps.

The reasons to stay alive are not equally clear to all the
sisters. My self-appointed job is to hold on to the survivors,
every last one, to force the will to live on them. Before I
sleep I patrol the edges of the cliffs we wander toward. I
lock the gates twice that are not my gates—the wrong key
for the lock, but I like to try, and loathe my trying. I think
I'm jealous of how near the terror they go, leaning way out
in the open with no net underneath, as if willing to fall in,
or willing to let whatever catches us catch them midair,
something external though not imposed in the same way
as my calling them back, my voice an interruption, and
powerless. They know I am not any more safe where I sit,
afraid that at any moment . . . and busy sorting photographs,
but if I lost them . . .

They are so flawless in black-and-white that you almost
miss what's missing. Abigail is lying on her belly with her
arms crossed in front of her to prop her halfway up. She
has on a dark shirt with large white polka dots, almost
covered by her long blond hair. Because of the way she
folds her legs back, you see her jeans and one cowboy boot
that isn't cropped out of the frame. Her expression is starkly
vacant, and off to the right. Neither the drift of reverie nor
the impatience with a long shoot registers. In another city,
Anne has flipped her hair so that the bangs are still falling,
and the wisp of hair that flies across her lips catches the
light as she turns her chin toward her shoulder to look into
the camera. She thinks of this pose, which will represent

her to casting directors and admirers across the country who have written seeking a reply. She feels enthusiasms other than those she has been hired to express.

Last year, at Thanksgiving, Anne was auditioning or something and couldn't take time off, but some friends and some family came. We had just moved into an old house that needed fixing up, far away from anything, and Abigail offered to prepare the food if I supplied the site. Outside, snow shrouded the hills. The pond was frozen and the ice perfect for skating. The kitchen had no floor yet, no oven —we'd plugged one in in the basement—the drywall needed to be taped. Abi had called to say how she was looking forward to being here. I'm looking forward to your food, I said. Are you up for this? My mother had conveyed the menu, always pleased to play the messenger between us. She had saved the turkey and venison to put on my list of things to do. I ironed the tablecloth and washed the plaster dust out of every glass and plate and serving dish I own. Apples hung on a corn-drying rack at the front door. The wood floors of the other rooms shone.

Abigail knocked the snow off her boots and came in the back door with an armload of pies in bakery boxes: apple, pumpkin, pecan, and strawberry-rhubarb. Her new husband carried a load of food prepared in my mother's baking dishes, letting my mother and her opera singer friend squeeze in the door in front of him, their arms loaded, too. Greetings all around, introductions of my friends to theirs, good cheer. The venison was barded and marinated, the turkey smoking. Something about the food was peculiar. My mother had clearly made everything but was pretending she hadn't. I watched her spoon the cranberries into a cut-glass bowl. One more charade. This new place was supposed to ward off fakery, but I played along. Abigail stood over the sink peeling potatoes, and I said, Look at all this great food! not knowing whether or not to ask about it. For Abigail, what does a holiday feast mean? Why did I ever let her talk me into this? To the person coming to terms with her addictions, what can a sister do to help? Shall I peel those? I offer, weakly.

This was all new to me. Abigail married Joe after tossing off an unbroken string of salesmen and jocks, and promptly checked herself into the hospital for six weeks to get help. No one would have thought of her as ill. She seemed well enough. Long trips to the bathroom after meals I attributed to hypercleanliness, excessive primping. She always looks beautiful. And distracted. Her answering machine is always on. She doesn't return my calls. I was surprised to hear from Mom that she was still intending to prepare Thanksgiving dinner at my house. "I'll peel the potatoes," she said. "Mom did everything but the stuffing. I made that." Again Mom had covered, pretending all was normal and well. She's used to it. We get together for her sake anyway, for the children, because it is a holiday and that is what a family does.

Dinner was finally ready. Everyone rushed with hot plates and dishes from the kitchen to the dining room and back for more. Our friends Jeff and Elizabeth poured water in the glasses and found a ladle for the gravy. Judson, my husband, ran to the basement oven for the cinnamon rolls. Elise, our second child, folded the edges of her new dress onto her lap and waited for the sweet potatoes to be passed.

Abigail's smile was bleary as she moved into the dining room from the living room, where she had been talking more than I had ever heard her talk.

She was letting us in on her therapy. This shit and that, she would say, sprawling across the table, her voice hard and loud. She couldn't stop talking that day any more than she could stop her stony silence the year before. Her stories started with partial memories of childhood, the seemingly harmless games and play times becoming ominously blighted as she connected them causally to who she had become. Through her therapy things were starting to make sense, and she seemed to want all of us to feel the recovery with her.

"I used to torment Anne in bed by making her play one more word game while she was trying to fall asleep." Abi rolled her eyes back in her head, exaggerating a young girl's tiredness. "I would say, Think of one more word, Anne, just one; she'd say, half sleeping, Jump. The word rhymes with jump. What does the word rhyme with? I would ask her. Jump, she'd say, falling asleep until I would shake her. Is it Bump? Is it Lump? I'd wake her up again. She was so tired I'd bully her awake. What is it, Anne? KANGAROO, she'd say." Abi howled with laughter. We all laughed, expecting another end to the story.

One by one all but Jeff left the table. We moved to games of chess, or picture books, or the stack of dishes. She was repeating herself. The wine turned up her volume. I sat down at the piano and started to play show tunes I knew Abi would remember, inviting Mom's baritone friend to join me. Abi came over to the piano bench and leaned against me, turning the pages of the music I was trying to read. "Do this one," she begged, and my fingers stumbled through "Someone to Watch over Me."

It was time for people to leave. Coats and platters gathered, we could not find Abi. The baby was asleep, so no one yelled, but several of us looked in all the places she could have been. The upstairs bathroom doors were all unlocked, no answer. We looked around outside in the dark. Finally, in the nursery, I found her standing over the crib staring down. When she saw me she took a step back and then slowly turned toward the door. I stood still until she passed me, then hurried to check the baby, who was sleeping on her back, her arms and legs spread. Mom met me on the stairs and in her chipper tone announced, "Abigail is fine. I told her this morning that if she felt blue she should stay close to the children." Joe pulled Abi out the front door gently. She resisted, laughing in a child's eerie voice. I stood at the door and watched her go.

I have been working on a painting of the daughters for our mother's fiftieth birthday. For reference I use photos of the three of us together at a wedding, or singly against the backdrop of a door, a fence, an artificial moon. Then there are the stories of women in threes I think might help. First Shakespeare's kingdom story: we are commanded to proclaim our father-love, by which orations the kingdom will be won. There is the story of three caskets—one made of gold, one silver, and one lead—that represent three choices for one man. Freud makes the caskets into women, into silence, into death, as always, or the drive for death, which a man longs to subdue. Or the tale of Blake's daughters of Albion, who, in their father's agony of self-division, says the poet, *unwind his mortal coil.* I've copied Blake's drawings from the library edition of "Jerusalem," along with Rubens's *Judgment of Paris*, and the Balthus studies of three bored-looking girls.

Three daughters is a plot: beginning, middle, and end. I control their composition, glancing in the mirror at my own pose. I'm not yet accomplished enough with weight and volume not to flatten them. I prop them up against my view, wishing to see more but unable to. Eight years now and we are only just beginning to unwrap our dressings. When I step back to look at the canvas, I recall how Gertrude Stein sat for over ninety sessions for Picasso before he smeared off her face and left town for the summer. It was impossible to look closely enough. She hardly counted the time it took. In her salon at 27, rue de Fleurus, Alice and Miss Mars devised a system for classifying women into three types: *femme décorative, femme d'intérieur*, and *femme intrigante*. The categories fail. We are our father's daughters. When Picasso came back to finish the portrait, Stein complained to him she didn't think it looked like her at all. "It will," he promised.

I call Abigail again. It's been over a year since we've been together. She's ready to talk, she thinks. She might be ready to come to my house again (though her voice rises at the end of her sentences) and sit for me while I draw and something will happen that isn't in the proofs. She might forgive me for the things I've said that were hurtful.

At the magazine rack tonight, in the all-night supermarket, Anne's character Vicky (the maverick twin) beams from the cover of *Soap Opera Digest*. I can tell it isn't really Anne, because she'd never dress like that. Her head is thrown back the way she laughs on the show. "Sex, Money, Power: How Girls From The Wrong Side Of The Tracks Get Ahead" says the headline, all the words capitalized, followed by the interviewer's queries:

What do people in Bay City fail to appreciate about Vicky?
Her sincerity and love for her sister. I think a majority of the characters think she's very self-centered. She just doesn't know how to express herself. She spends her time coming up with schemes, trying to prove to people that she's not the way they think she is.

Would you rather play one sister than the other?
No. I like playing two people. I'm very fortunate. It's hard work, it's a challenge. I'm glad they're both back.

I lean over my empty cart in the cereal aisle. The children are asleep at home. I've left them alone. Hardly anyone is shopping at this hour. The fish case is empty except for ice, and the deli counter's wiped down. My husband is in Texas. The painting is too hard to finish. Maybe I'll stay here all night. Maybe I'll just lie down on the floor for a minute. Three Graces, muses; three-headed monster. In the masters' paintings three women rise from the sea or dance in a forest, holding their hands aloft, bathed in light. They acquire wings.

I have my sketches. We are all in the same frame this time, like the figures in Andrei Rublev's *Old Testament Trinity*, who appear to be angels staring into the same bowl. Or nothing like the Trinity at all. I can't hold the view of us all together inside me. Here is the Apple of Discord, here the Zephyr balm. If I am part of the image, who will save us? *This is not your painting*, a voice says.

We are pulling out to the edges of the page. How unnatural we look. The daughters have all waded into the river that fills in between us. *We are the children of God, and it has not appeared as yet what we shall be.*

3 /

*W*hen we ran out of money, the paintings worked like magic. My father would take one down from the pair of nails it hung on and would carry it —his face close to the portrait's face—to his creditor's car. He related the few facts he had been told about the artist's life, a name changed from Hinshaw to Henshaw, sent to Europe for formal training by the disapproving father of a Brown County girl, a barren witch for a second wife. Then, ceremoniously, under the cloud of repossession or eviction, he would turn the picture around in the natural light before the man drove off, the "collateral" padded with a blanket or propped in the trunk on top of the spare tire. It took those last months of my father's life, when he was nearly frantic for financial recovery, to get down to the bare walls. All the oils and the larger pastels, the portrait of the old black sailor and the one of the girl with the bow in her hair went to the landlord, who already held most of the collection hostage, for six months of unpaid rent.

The ownership of the pictures is still in question. Maybe my father did buy them finally, after failing to sell them to anyone else. Maybe he never let them go. He said once that he was planning to make a fair offer for the lot, and in all these years no one has ever come to claim the few we've kept. Maybe we have moved one too many times for anyone to keep track. The paintings were put into my father's care by two women dressed like men who lived together in Florida and occasionally in Ohio in a house without the right kind of light, my father told me. They had bought the works as an investment and made him the paintings' agent. I remember one woman's taper cut and the other's pure white, evenly trimmed bangs. One had flattened her breasts somehow, it appeared to me, as I was working to grow mine, and so seemed unencumbered by what I had been taught were women's roles and duties. Prone instead to male cares, male freedoms, they were as dismissive of children as men were, though they made a show of goodwill to us children the first Christmas we celebrated as a family. They sat in the living room like a pair of adopted and distant aunts, exchanging witticisms with my father.

I was fourteen years old when we first drove to pick up the collection at the shop where the oils had been cleaned and the pastels had been newly placed in huge gold frames with black velvet matting. Behind the glass I could make out cities with domed centers and rivers that narrowed under ancient bridges into the fog. I still have the drawing of the Chrysler Building, soaring toward the clouds, its confetti lights shining down on the trafficked New York streets. But most of the works were portraits of people exotic and woeful enough to be our ancestors, or even gods. What a gift it was, I thought, for a girl who wanted to paint to have a master's works to live with in her own house. Along the hallway upstairs, across from the dining-room windows, on the blank walls of the living room, my father arranged and rearranged them. Surely I would learn the angle of jaw, the lips' elusive edge, the shadow under the brow that made a flat page dimensional with life.

American Impressionism had not yet been commodified; the price list the women had printed seemed arbitrarily exorbitant for the relatively unknown Glen Cooper Henshaw. There were over one hundred works in all, to be sold as a collection only, and so initially, in keeping with the terms of sale, they were not sold but moved with us from house to house like a troupe of minstrels jostled but unflappable.

Then one day in Atlantic City a black woman my mother had met at church saw in them the story of our lives. We did not believe her altogether then, but when I unpacked the few remaining pictures to hang them in the house where I now live, I thought of that woman's warning and wondered what I risked.

It was the paintings that first drew her to my mother, Jelma said. My parents regularly visited a racially mixed Baptist church that on Sunday nights brought in rock or jazz musicians who testified to dramatic conversion experiences. They were singing for their Lord. The group would paly, then pass the plate, talking through a two-minutes gospel in closing for the visitors lured in by the thick bass rumble that pulsed through the surrounding neighborhood. Jelma was hiding out from her ex-husband, now openly homosexual, who had brought his lovers home. She had settled temporarily a block from the church where she had been delivered, as she told it, from a life as a psychic that began as a young girl when her mother had started charging for her "gift." Her offhand observations had the ring of truth; they, in fact, came true. She didn't even have to touch a woman's hand to see her knot of suffering. Smell his breath, she told her mama, it's an omen. A man's boss is about to fire him when his children walk down the opposite side of the street.

Gifts or perceptions, she read the images for clues, the spirit voices clustering in dreams. Waking signs had not yet turned off, though she'd given her soul to Christ. We had first seen her driving through town in an old school bus painted blue, in which she gathered unattended children and other of Atlantic City's early castoffs. One day the bus appeared on the street in front of our house and the pictures began to talk to her.

She had walked into the kitchen and started snapping the ends off beans, until the whole bag was finished and washed and thrown in the copper-bottomed pot with the new potatoes and ham my mother was simmering for dinner. They sat down after eating that night with their Bibles, marking the tissue pages gently so the ink would not run through, reading between passages the doctrine of predestination right on through to righteous liberty. *In Christ there is no Jew nor Greek, no male nor female, slave nor free*, I heard them read aloud, and believed it. The image of a different world rose up in me the way the figures in the pictures haunted Jelma. It was the first night she tried to sleep in our guest room that my mother heard her talking back to them.

In that room my father had hung the portrait of the painter's second wife. She was wearing a white gown with light brushstrokes of lace along the collar's edge. She hovered in the center of a dark room. Only her face was fully illumined from a light source off to the left of the canvas. Her brown hair and the shadowy edges of her dress nearly blended in with the background, so that she appeared bodiless, floating in the picture's space. Jelma called her Carolyn when they spoke. The two sides of Carolyn's face were noticeably unmatched. One eyebrow was raised slightly, as if she was worried, and the other eye smiled, the two combined making her seem to mock and doubt whomever it was she saw. Wherever you stood in the room, she saw you. They were not friendly dialogues between Jelma and the painting but accounts of torment in marriage, torment to come, torment from which even the dead are not exempt.

Jelma would lock the door and try to cast the painter's wife's spirit from the room, furiously, in the middle of the night, while the rest of us slept. Carolyn touched her face to wake her, and they wrestled through the night until dawn, the figure metamorphosing from woman to dwarfish man to the lizard-like shape int he lower corner of the canvas where the paint had begun to peel. Carolyn, too, had been a medium who, for all her concert with the spirit world, had not found her way to final rest. She needed Jelma, she insisted, to arbitrate her passage, but not until she had spent the curse she carried like a longed-for child.

At breakfast one morning, unsteadily, falling from the middle of the night's vertiginous loops and whorls into our family chatter, Jelma told us, "Images are the resting place of spirits." She could not butter her toast, her hand shook so. "You must get these pictures out of the house before it is too late." My father had already gone to the office where he was working to lease land from farmers to drill oil wells. "She'll destroy your family, beginning with your husband, one by one," she said to my mother in a whisper. "The son next." She meant it. There was more, Margo told my mother that morning: Carolyn's threats and curses foresaw much of what we have lived out. But my mother can't remember most of what she said.

I had crept upstairs to peer into the room with Margo's revelations fresh in my mind. The woman in the painting seemed eerily calm, her skin loosely rounded over her bones. She stood as still as the dresser and bedside table I went in the room once a week to dust. Stiller than that. I looked for more. She was sneering now, her shoulders pinned back by the dark enshrouding her. I made the bed neatly, folding the sheet over the blanket edge while I kept my eyes from blinking by squinting hard.

The difference between Margo's range of cognizance and mine, which hours of attention could not amend, was a lesson in the many possible ways of seeing. Leonardo da Vinci found in the sense of sight several different qualities, a family of attributes that contribute to perception, and so to interpretation: darkness, light, solidity, color, form, position, motion and rest, distance and propinquity. Each attribute in turn has its own qualities. Take the last pair's common traits as observed by Harold Gatty in *Finding Your Way on Land and Sea*: "Objects look closer than they really are when you're looking up- or downhill; across water, snow, or flat sand; or when the air is clear." You know this to be so. "Objects look farther away than they actually are when the light is poor, the color of an object blends with its surrounding, or the ground is undulating."

The other day I overheard my children discussing a drawing one of them had hung on the pantry wall. The older one loved the way the lines went all the way to the edge of the page. "But there's lightning in the center of your house," he said. "That's not lightning." The younger one was adamant. "Those are yellow stairs!" The puzzle of interpretation starts in the kitchen before we turn five. One time we see the sudden illuminating flash, another the irrhythmic path of our ascents and descents. Perhaps the light is poor, the object moving at too fast a rate. We are suspended in the unclear air, where there are more than eight aspects to sight. Da Vinci accounts for the way the eyes take hold and does not attempt to broach the subject of the mystical Brailles and ciphers that remain beyond our view.

What Jelma saw was triggered by the images on the canvas, and by her intercourse with the unseen. I have no doubt that the windows of the visible open onto vistas of invisibility. Or that Jelma, because of her experience, must have sensed in my father's dissembling, in his wild unhappiness and stormings from the family table, the catastrophe to come, which, in her own voice, was unspeakable. What she kept asserting she saw in front of her, speaking with the authority and intonation of the dead, was a woman's ghost she could not exorcise. The paintings needed to be sold at once, and something purchased to depose their power in our lives.

We could embrace the curse or turn away from it, invite blessing, or close and lock our gates. In this deliberate choice an image is often implicated, for standing in the way, for reminding us, for coaxing trouble, for transmuting the elements of salvation.

The disbelieving, too, are not immune. There is a spear that is said to have pierced the side of Christ. It hung in a glass case in the Hofberg Library in Vienna, where Hitler would stand some days for hours on end, inviting the spear's power to overwhelm him, worked by the spear's presence into a trance. Trevor Ravenscroft, in his book *The Spear of Destiny*, describes the self-eclipsing effects of the spear on Hitler:

Adolf Hitler stood . . . like a man in a trance, a man over whom some dreadful magic spell had been cast. His face was flushed and his brooding eyes shone with an alien emanation. He was swaying on his feet as though caught up in some totally inexplicable euphoria. The very space around him seemed enlivened with some subtle irradiation, a kind of ghostly ectoplasmic light. His whole physiognomy and stance appeared transformed as if some mighty Spirit now inhabited his very soul, creating within and around him a kind of evil transformation of its own nature and power.

Hitler believed that Constantine had grasped the spear in his hand when he conquered Rome in A.D. 312. The spear had borne forty-five Roman emperors to triumph. He ached to possess such destiny. To oppose God and win, to have the will to destroy the very likeness of His image. His people. When he marched into Vienna he took the spear into his possession. He prayed to that spear, believing that the powers of evil flocked to him. The spear was the site of their swarming. It hung without a flutter of power on the wall of St. Katherine's Church in Nuremberg, where Hitler knelt down before it. After falling into the hands of the Allies the day Hitler committed suicide, the spear hangs again under heavy guard in Vienna, an object of occult devotion.

When we still lived in the beach house in Ocean City, a deacon in the Baptist Church bought one of the larger paintings for enough cash to cover our heating bill, and another for a short-term loan so my father could commute between New York City and the shore. My father was sharing an office on Wall Street with the other principals in his current part-time venture. He played piano for an Off Broadway show at night. On Sunday mornings he would pull into the parking lot just in time to direct the church choir. He was perpetually exhausted with effort, the end in sight—but not yet, any day now.

He was searching for a $10 billion loan for Mexico, collateralized by oil, for which he had been guaranteed one percent, or $100 million, as his finder's fee. His partnership in the Red Parrot Club was nearly sealed, the new design drawn with leather banquettes and man-sized feathers. He had a buyer on the hook for the Empire State Building and was flying to Texas on Sheik ———'s private jet to confirm the commitment. We were to pronounce his title *Shake*, not *Sheek*; he did not want to catch us making that mistake again. *Shake*, Susan, he is not Omar Sharif. At a folding card table in the downstairs family room, he had set up a telephone and a makeshift file system, a Rolodex and a jar of monogrammed pens. He would draw the vertical blinds against the sun's glare on the sand. He did not want to look at the ocean just now, he must sort through his small slips of paper for the phone number, where is it? My brother bounded down the stairs three at a time. "Nathan, you jackass, keep quiet in this house, as though an idiot could think with you pounding down those stairs." Jackass? We were used to his temper, but not its coarse vocabulary. Nathan needed him to play the song he was going to sing for his audition, but not now. We knew our father could be soothed if he would come to the piano to play the old hymns, the show tunes we sang with our hands resting on his shoulders.

As the deal flow quickened, the flurry of calls, wires, his take in the pipeline, he borrowed a neighbor's van so we could all drive to Long Island to look for a proper house. The real estate would overlook the Sound. It was a clear, bright Saturday. After each mansion we reviewed in detail the gardens and pool, the outbuildings and servants' wing, extra bedrooms, linen closets, the arrangement of the furniture and artworks, where we would place ours, kitchen appliances, built-ins, the automated lights and alarms. We looked at the houses as only those can who have seen such luxury from the outside, as visitors, with the pretense of deserving.

Not until we had dropped my father off on a corner near Times Square, with one small Sportsac of weekend belongings, did the houses seem unreal. What will you eat? I remember asking him. He was growing thinner and blamed it on his pace, his working through the night to finally close the deal. I will eat oatmeal, he said—to confirm his wholesome appetites, his self-neglect? I knew he had only the money he had borrowed from his children in his pocket. We did not have enough among us to pay for his bus fare home. I'm going to find you the perfect prom dress, he promised Abigail over his shoulder.

The images of that period in our lives have all been sorted through again and again, like a deck of cards, for what we had evidently, blindly overlooked. Then the cards told tales of great wealth to come, great journeys that would shape great lives. What did the paintings know that we did not? In a short time the world would . . . just around the corner, behind that low-hung cloud *Success* was planning to catch us up in its mists!

That Christmas, the year of the hunt for adequate quarters, 1979—the year I was married, the family arrived at our apartment early in the morning. I had made cinnamon rolls; we had a small, fragrant tree. Tea poured, we sat on the floor to open gifts. My brother and sisters had made fantastic animals of clay or woven bright yarns on lap-sized looms. I have no recollection of what I gave. It is my father's gifts we talk about now. For each of us he had printed in his flowing script on large sheets of heavy paper the present he had not had time to purchase yet. They were rolled up, and he had tied red ribbons around each one, which he stood to hand to us, individually, with instructions as to the order in which we were to read the gifts aloud. My mother read hers first. He had given her a family cruise to wherever she wanted to take us all. Nathan was going to get diving gear. Abigail and Anne had certificates for flight school, valid when they turned sixteen. I was to buy, at my father's expense, the camera my mother must have told him I wanted. He gave Judson, my new husband, an actual Commodores album, which we played over and over that day, my mother inviting my father to dance, and he obliging, keeping his eyes closed as he pressed her against his thigh and, with his hand supporting the small of her back, leaned her out away from him, then swept her back in close.

What we can't fathom, looking back, is the credulity that we displayed on that day. For his sake we spent the afternoon planning, checking sizes, poring over maps. It must have been our unacknowledged doubt that fired his extravagance (money was no object for the first time ever), our complicity. We wanted what he gave us—the high hopes, the impossibility. None of us pressed him then, or ever after, to come through.

It's not easy to let go of the picture of a family in a beautiful house filled with ancestral heirlooms, the great talent of the father and flawlessness of the mother, the children's careless laughter. We would have three more Christmases with Nathan before his accident. First the father, Jelma had warned us, then the son. We burn the false images like graven idols, the relations we had to them screaming in the fire. Turning from a lie we can search for a true thing. Saying that truth aloud in front of the mirage defeats the phantasms, but at what cost? Recover from the lie, and you must then heal from the truth.

To ward off her illusions, eight years after my father and brother died, my mother drove to Atlantic City, to reclaim the paintings from her former landlord. We had lost them but had not escaped the curse; there was no reason not to try to get them back. She had sent letters itemizing the artwork and jewelry, the furniture and accessories he had taken when he locked the family out of his house, finally, the paintings of less value to him than the next tenant's cash. My father had been months away from dying then. There were doctor's bills my mother was working to pay but none of the anticipated gush of wealth. My mother had called to tell the landlord she was on her way. She had not consulted a lawyer, but one of the boys she'd taught in Sunday school was now a local cop and she had asked him for advice. He could not involve himself directly, of course, he told her, but would do whatever he could within the boundaries of the law.

She and my sister Anne, off duty from her soap opera, stormed into the landlord's offices, unannounced, and said they would not leave until he gave them back the pictures, NOW. Surely the inventory he had taken when he had put their suitcases on the street had covered any back rent. A play to his compassion, to his sense of fairness. Her engagement ring, the ruby-and-diamond pin from her great-grandmother, the piano. Everything they owned. Surely he did not want legal action. They had been too desperate then for any redress. "You don't want us to call the local newspaper, do you?" On his intercom he told his wife, in the adjoining office, to please inform the police that he had two trespassers on the premises whom he'd like placed under arrest immediately. "Ladies, that's the past. I have hung the paintings over the years in my rental properties," he told my mother, "in which my tenants pay their rent." Anne was not acting now, though her pitch was theatrical, the names she had for him coming easily: who didn't know the difference between art and the bottom of his shoe, whose children reveled in the mud outside like swine, whose wife's skinny neck . . . As they were shown in by the landlord's wife, the police held their handcuffs ready, stopping short of the offenders. A look at each other, before the younger officer looked down at his buttons, and away.

For my mother, who had lost her husband, and then her son, her things, her cache of memories to revision, and the supposition of her own future health, the paintings were a tangible object that marked a missing time and had value because of this, and because she could have sold them someday or given them back. For Anne, the paintings were a part of lost childhood. They were the one thing she could think of that might possibly—oh, please, God—relieve her mother's sorrow.

Whatever it was that Margo saw, and heard, and wrestled with—lightning or yellow stairs, demons or our family's deceit—we still combat it. It is not specific to a single site. It is not flesh and blood but the steady force of darkness: what we might look at and not see, what we might blindly desire. What we hold on to like crazy that eventually may devour us. Finding out requires a willingness to adjust our eyes to the light. The curse of the father, the way I heard it, visits the children. Visits. But it doesn't live here.

There are three things that will not be satisfied,
Four that will not say "Enough":
The nether-world, and the barren womb,
Earth that is never satisfied with water,
And fire that never says, "Enough."

— PROVERBS 30:15–16

4 / 𝓘f to assuage a craving (to slake a *true* thirst), if to satisfy a need requires us to name the need accurately, it must also require us to draw the need out of its habit of wanting. The netherworld of the family past engorges on its members' deficiency. The farther in you go, the greater the renouncing. Soon you will accuse your mother! Imagine the files of blame since Freud. Fire has such a disposition. Insatiable as long as it is fed, it burns. A child burns because she cannot relieve her parents' learned neglect. One must count one's satisfactions. Couldn't she rehearse, instead of her regret, this winning smile, a prize for the past, for survival! He does so well, considering. You were a happy child, dear. Applause,

cheers, in the absence of which the delicate acquired appetite for emptiness enlarges.

It was no secret when they married that the girl's family
was too good for the people the boy came from. He had
grown up in the rooms behind the backwater grocery; its
gas pumps and live bait, its soda cooler and canned goods
were the façade of a small house filled with overstuffed
furniture and an electric organ. On the walls hung three
pictures: one, a waterscape on black velvet which the boy
had bought his parents for a present as a young man, hung
over the deep blue horsehair sofa. The other two were three-
dimensional flowers made of dyed pale green shells and
coral-colored seahorses glued onto a background of glit-
tering sand. The living room looked out over the northern-
most inlet of Lake Webster, where his father had anchored
a floating dock from which he rented a few aluminum row-
boats to fishermen. The rooms of the house absorbed the
meaty sweat of the customer's bodies, the father's cigarettes,
and the oily tang of gasoline and lye soap.

What amazed the girl's family, who spent half the year
in Washington, D.C., and half in Indiana, was how the boy,
raised in that environment, had taught himself the organ
and piano as well as anyone in six counties. By the age of
twelve he was playing organ on Sunday mornings for the
church on the edge of town. Summers he could fill the big
wooden auditorium at the Epworth Forest campgrounds
with the sound of organ pipes that outdid all the voices
rising in a single hymn out over the lake. The anomaly of
his great talent issued like a sudden and devouring storm
across the Midwestern cornfields. It was disproportionate
to the landscape, neither contained nor local. It lived and

would return somewhere else. But for the time being, the boy was its vessel and, as such, shouldered the appraisal others usually lavished on a saint or a freak.

It must have been her family's perception of his family's disadvantage that gave the girl's wishes such force, such an absolute ring of necessity in the boy's mind. Over the gorge between her privilege and his relative poverty he would work to construct an elaborate makeshift bridge. She and her twin sister had traveled across the United States as children and had been pampered with matching souvenirs. They each had cashmere sweaters in every pastel color, with coordinating pastel skirts, and pearls with pearl clasps. Their house was the substantial brick Victorian surrounded by a wide white porch on top of the hill in the Noble County seat. Her parents owned the Republican newspaper and wrote the editorials that sparked the rival columns of their Democrat competition. There were campaign dinners and election parties. While the boy's father when drunk would beat his wife and children with his shaving strop, the girl's father drank his cocktails gracefully, as a social elixir.

As children, the girl and her identical twin would perch on the back of the baby-blue Olds convertible for local parades, tossing campaign buttons and handing out bumper stickers for congressmen whose chief aide and speechwriter their father was. The months he was home from the capital, there were constituents' hands to shake and the need for ever more votes. The sisters kept their ankles crossed. In their matching French braids with red-white-and-blue ribbons they must not forget to smile and wave.

By the time the twins were in high school, they had cut their hair into look-alike short bobs. The girl remembers her days centering on the boy, who in a neighboring town was lettering in varsity basketball. The earliest photograph she has of him is a school newspaper black-and-white. He is poised to shoot, bent slightly at the knees and waist, with a basketball in his hands at shoulder height. His eyes are focused intently upward on an invisible hoop, and he is just about to score when he is caught, motionless.

In her mind still is the clearer picture of him at the keyboard, the sound encircling them, excluding the world at the edges of the notes as he played. He reaches athletically for the lowest organ pedals. He walks down the bass scale with his heel-toe motion to connect the notes of the B flat major fugue. It is the first night of the districtwide Methodist Youth Rally. It should begin with a formally complex tone that sheds any of the common trappings of low-church choruses the participants might be bringing with them. The music would elevate their worship. It would clear room for the Spirit of God. The boy could draw the crowd from the rumbling bars of chords on the lower register all the way up into the epiphanic rills and arpeggios—the stops shifting from brass to strings to the hollow flute sound of the closing measures he pulls quickly without losing his touch on the keys—the volume heightening, the young woman on the podium spreading her arms for people to rise and sing hymn number 353 in a higher key. He modulates effortlessly into the introduction, and the myriad voices that occupy the hall, tentative at first, then coaxed by the organ's ripening fullness, fill in with confidence.

From where she is standing on the platform, the girl can see the way his body complements the instrument. His head is bowed slightly forward over his spread hands as he feels the music take hold of the crowd. How will she hear a word the speaker says? Whatever the challenge presented, she resolves, she will make it her own, and will make the boy with the blond hair and blue eyes and the gift of music love her. After the service, when the youth pastor introduces them, she thinks to herself, "I will never forget how to pronounce this boy's name. Heche: like the letter H, with a little wind in front of it." He is there that night with another girl, but she goes back to her room and writes in her diary, like a charm, that he will call her, which he does.

From then on they were pretty much steadies, though she was always needlessly jealous of Judy Coons, who could sing so beautifully, and of Donna Fiddler, who also loved him for a while. They enrolled at Indiana University together, she to become a teacher, he pre-med, full scholarship. His music was a current with no ready outlet then, but full of promise, the world becoming available in its first heady doses.

Things were coming fast for them, and they rushed it. The girl's mother wore a pink pillbox hat at their wedding, the summer after their freshman year. The bridesmaids wore wide pink straw hat brims that left the crowns of their heads showing. They stepped down the aisle in full, fifties-style organdy dresses. He in his navy tux, she in her gown. Had it begun yet? Someone had removed the perfect couple from the top of the wedding cake, so that the bride and groom could carve and feed the heavy frosting to each other with their arms interlocking for the camera. Had she known then, would she have hurried so? Her mother asked if she was sure. "I just want to get married," the girl protested. Had his father and mother—impelled by their immigrant parents, who had fled from the deprivations of their early homes—set his course? As long as fire's fed it burns. Light a match in a dry field. Set a single milkweed pod on fire untended, and the wind's effortless licking . . .

I was born at the end of my parents' sophomore year of college and they took turns attending classes with me in tow for two years. I came along as predicted by my mother's mother, whose namesake I am, a year and a month after their June wedding. Naturally, I was unplanned and dreaded and the start of something (a family), and the purported end of something else. A first child of near-children, I was showered with love once they saw me. I was a proof of how good they could be together. A composite of their noses and eyes, his long middle toe, her easy way with sleep, favoring them both, miraculous, I was a tiny vocal symptom of their wholeness.

My mother's friends from that time still introduce me as the first baby in the world. As they helped to feed and entertain me, I was what it would be like for them someday, a trial run, an inevitable culmination of the dangerous and mysterious sexual whirl. On graduation day I picked my mother out of the crowd in her cap and gown as she went forward for her diploma. My mother's parents held a parasol over my head to shade me from the hot sun. My father, short a few credits, couldn't graduate, but had his medical school acceptance in hand, and a Phi Beta Kappa pin. His parents had arrived late and stood in the shade of the bleachers until after the ceremonies.

After graduation, we moved to a small apartment with blue-striped draperies on a busy road in Cleveland so that he could attend what was then called Western Reserve Medical School. In the center of his heaviest textbook, on acetate pages, the male and female bodies could be peeled back in layers, skin first, then muscles, organs, nerves, and bones. All the way in there were two different kinds. I could not read the names of any of the parts, but I would recognize the order of the intricate anatomies when I saw them.

Daddy comes home early one evening from the lab. Something has gone wrong. It has been half a year of study, he is tired, he told them today that was it.

"Without even talking to me?" my mother wants to know, baffled. "Is it too much pressure? You're doing so well; the scholarship." There is no plan particularly, but he is adamant and the decision is final.

"We'll stay in Ohio." He sounds more certain than he must feel. "And I'll get a job; it's about time. There are some shady things going on there I want nothing to do with," he finishes. What things he doesn't say. She can't take his decision back. She can't even ask him to reconsider. What kind of shady things, my mother barely wonders, angry not to have married a doctor.

It is Sunday after church and my mother slides the pot roast out of the oven. First she spoons the meat onto the platter, then the potatoes and carrots. She ladles some fatty liquid from the pan over the meat and carries it into the dining room. She sets it down in front of my father and lays out serving spoons beside the frozen cranberry salad and the cottage cheese. For weeks she has been feeling helpless and trying not to. She has a new policy—out of the situation a life principle has arisen she feels sure will work for her—you can either make a bad situation worse by letting your unhappiness show, or you can make it better by being happy anyway. So far, so good. This will be a fine day.

Rain drizzles all morning. My mother's cousin and her doctor husband are joining us for dinner. We have bowed our heads and given thanks for the food.

The man I call Uncle Jack is talking seriously about how stressful the first year of medical school can be. He remembers how persistently he wanted to quit, no sleep at all for weeks, how everyone felt that way sometime in the course of the program, don't you think? "But this passes, for most of us." He laughs a little and chucks me on the chin. "So, Don, how are you holding up? Anatomy? Chem.?" My mother must have told them. Uncle Jack had attended the same medical school my father did. She is looking at my father, who is finishing chewing. We are all waiting for his answer.

"I guess it hasn't hit me yet, Jack," my father answers, wiping his mouth at the corners. "I've always loved a challenge." He was so good at it; the rhythm of the conversation was intact. He steered the discussion to one of their mutual professors. Maybe it wasn't really final yet and he had thought it over, after all. He cleans his plate of the last bite of food and places his soiled napkin beside his fork. Jack doesn't push. My mother excuses herself to clear the table for dessert.

Now she will quit her job teaching and work harder to have more children. They have been trying desperately for a year with no results. She has the names all chosen. They will find a more spacious home on a quiet street. There are rosebushes of all colors growing in the back yard. They pin them into my hair. My father is going to sell insurance. I help him stack the different forms.

On the way to places (sometimes we went along to keep

him company on his calls) I would sit beside my father on the front seat with my hand tucked under his leg. He liked me there and would quiz me on the orchestra instruments as they played on the classical music station. "Is that a French horn or an oboe, do you think?" he asked. Most brass and woodwinds I could not confuse, but I had to listen especially carefully to these.

"That high-sounding instrument, what is that?"

"A flute?" I said it like a question, just in case. That one was simple.

"Good, now listen to how the flute takes the theme the violins just played and repeats it!" Then he would turn the volume all the way down and say, "There, can you hum the tune for me?" Where I fell off the melody he could always prop my small voice up with his until I was back on key. My mother was proud of his perfect pitch. I would ask him for a middle C sometimes out of the blue, to remind her of his musical flawlessness. It was a test we could never tell if he was failing.

We sang along with the songs on the Christian radio station—all the verses of the hymns I still know by heart. What amazed me as a little child sitting there beside him all tucked in was my father's pure harmonizing tenor. How could he know where the thirds or fifths fit up next to the melody? "How does that work?" I asked him. "You know the parts to every song!"

"If you listen closely enough to one note," he answered, "it will tell you all the others." I heard his voice blend and saw the pleasure and conviction he sang with, especially the words of the hymns about Jesus. "Beneath the Cross of Jesus," "What a Friend We Have in Jesus," *Jesus, Jesus,*

Jesus, sweetest name I know, fills my every longing, keeps me singing as I go. He had a medley of children's choruses we sang. And my mother sang along, too.

"I don't have the voice your daddy does," she apologized. "But I sound okay if I sing softly with him."

They throw themselves into church life, helping with the senior-high Sunday-school class. My father plays the piano for Sunday nights and special services. People come over after the evening vespers for popcorn and to sing around the piano. They even take a trip to Niagara Falls with a few other young couples, discussing doctrine and the possibility of breaking off to form a smaller, theologically more sound church of their own. The joy of their new friendships is fueled by the diligence of their faith. The women sleep in one hotel room after they have rolled each other's hair. In the room next door the men argue over the Rapture. I hear them through the walls. In the morning at breakfast they have their Bibles open to Revelation, trying to make literal sense of the phantasmagoric vision of John. I am listening quietly to every word.

As I'm beginning to read, it is these stories that strike me with awe. There are saints in white robes at a golden altar who worship a lamb that bleeds. There is a woman balancing on the moon and wearing only the sun for clothes. She is about to have a baby that a great red dragon with seven heads and a tail that sweeps the stars away is famished for. My parents are for the first time in their lives what they call truly spiritually alive.

At the wax museum my mother lingers over the North American Indian display. The others have gone on ahead. Depicted in one section is the ritual enactment of a child sacrifice. "They believed with their whole hearts that it

would make their crops grow if they gave up the most im-
portant possession they could conceive," my mother tells
me years later, far from where she stood then. "And I
thought—looking from the horrified expression on the wax
child's face to the knife in the medicine man's hand—that
is how much I love God. If at that moment God had demanded, as they thought their gods had, that I sacrifice my
child, I would have done it." She fixes her gaze on the half
circle of unlit candles that line the site of the altar.

Her friend comes back to get her. They are going for
hamburgers and Cokes, and then on to the next attraction.
"Nancy, c'mon. You don't want to miss Niagara Falls, do
you?"

She prays and prays for another baby. She bows down
and lets her lips silently shape her prayer as Hannah, Sam-
uel's mother, prayed. Because one is never enough. Because
this one I have is so dear to me. *This is my vow: If you will
give a son to me, I will surely give him back. My Lord, I am
a woman oppressed of spirit.* And then, suddenly, my mother
is pregnant again at last, and she goes into the hospital in
her crisp blue maternity suit and pillbox hat and white
gloves, and baby Cynthia is born, but they cannot bring her
home yet.

"She has a small hole in her heart," my grandmother
tries to make me understand. I am not permitted to visit
the intensive-care ward of the hospital. Children carry
germs. My mother heads directly upstairs when she comes
home, and after supper I am allowed to tiptoe into her
bedroom very quietly to say good night. Her round belly is
flat again. She has her hand up by her long brown hair on
the pillow. She seems to be staring at the flowered wallpaper
near her window.

"May I see the baby tomorrow?" I whisper. She does not answer for a long time. The bones that stretch between her neck and shoulders rise a little when she swallows.

"We will have to see," she says, not taking her eyes off the flowers.

My father has been talking with the doctors. There is nothing they can do. So many complications surround the heart's condition. After a month and eight days, during the night, the baby loses consciousness and slips away.

One thirst is greedy for another. What wants rain wants more than rain. What wants love. What wants, the very source stanched at the mouth—this trickle is never enough. Is it a disease to want so? Is death's want the abject emblem of this greed? My mother calls in her dead. After her husband was buried, and her son, she developed a keen interest in mortality. This month alone, keeping track, there was the highway accident of her neighbor on the way to her parents' house, her friend's lover's murder by his deranged son. A grandmother's prayer was granted for her own decease. I tell her of Beau, who, wading in his older sister's boots in the river behind their house, was swallowed by the flooded current while the other children played, unaware. Wherever we look, it's there.

The first night in our new old house, exhausted with the move in pouring rain, my husband and I are wakened in the middle of the night by a pounding on our front door. We live down a long dirt road, so someone would have to have wanted to come this far this late in the storm. Here he is, dripping and gasping. "There's been an accident at the end of your drive. Someone took the curve too fast. I didn't try to pull him out of the jeep. Thought I should call

the sheriff first," the stranger blurts. He couldn't tell if the
driver was conscious or not, or how long ago it had happened. The motor is still running. Lights on. "Could you
come with me, please?" He is stomping his feet nervously
on the cardboard box spread on the hallway floor as a makeshift rug. We show him where the phone is while my husband and I tear into our jackets and boots and follow the
stranger's lights into the torrential rain.

The boy in the jeep is the age of my brother, whose
body I was too afraid to claim. He took off from the curve
of the road at a high speed into a tree. Is it my task to pull
his headless body from the wreckage? There are men
dressed for the weather with probing lights. My husband
has offered to help and been sent away. They reach in
through the broken window to turn off the ignition, then
the lights of the crumpled jeep, then begin to pry open the
door, blinded by the rain, hurrying. I fold up on the seat of
our car, shaking. If we could have a little *mercy*. This fire
turned down-O. Leave our heads on, leave our heart's need.
The minute I get up out of the grave, whack. It is me, dear
Lord, asking for my body to be met in air.

It is not until early morning, when I have gone down
to inspect the tree, that I find the boy's skateboard embel-
lished with monster heads and rock group decals, which I
haul around in the back of my car for days before I pass it
to the road crew who comes to clean up the debris. I was
going to take it to his mother, who is my new neighbor,
they tell me, but I have less than most to say to her.

I tell my mother about the boy at the end of our drive
and she cries again. Any rumored sorrow aggravates her
own. She takes out her pictures of Nathan and weeps, calling up flattened episodes from the family past; like hand-

tinted photographs, the color is unreal. Her grief swells on the anniversaries of their births and deaths. She forces herself to think a long way back. None of the loss, no facts. "I will never stop loving your father," she says. "Most things in life you just can't help."

It's better if the dead come for the weekend so she doesn't have to miss work. She can spend the morning cooking for them. She can make up the beds for us to sleep in so that they don't stay the night. (She has dreamed them again.) None of us can soothe her suffering, any more than we are able to possess the full range of her abjection—this ever-enlarging temple into which she flings her inconsolability. Weren't they all she had? Aren't we, the survivors, lovely but elusive, ongoing? She will feed us, too, the fruit of her hard grieving. The fidelity of her conspicuous labor to sustain them is never enough. They appear disfigured, their faces hideously bloated. Their shrieks shed like molting insects in the dream's air.

After Cynthia died, we moved out to the country where the Amish people lived, and three years later, in April of 1965, Nathan was born. The pastor of the small breakaway church and my father had agreed to purchase forty acres together, on which they would build their families' houses away from the lure of the world. They had located a site on top of a hill on which there was a clearing in the middle of a woodland parcel. First came Nathan, then Abigail, then Anne. My mother kept the family fed with rations from intermittent jobs my father found, or with charity. I had a vegetable garden the rabbits and groundhogs ate most of, and some marigolds. I had a room of my own, where I read or played chess with David, the neighbor boy, who was just a year younger than I was. Or I wrote and illustrated poems like the ones I had read in the heavy pages of my great-grandmother's collections of English Romantic and Hoosier poets. By twelve I had developed a distaste for James Whitcomb Riley's singsong rhyme. I could smell the stagnant backwater of an Indiana lake in his graying lines, in contrast to the sweet-smelling, unquenchable strivings of the young dead. What I wanted from poems, what I still want, my favorite poems want, too.

The neighbors always blamed my father for the fire. It was a steamy August. He started it in the morning after the dew burned off. From an upstairs window I saw him fan the cinders, feeding the sparks handfuls of seed heads. The neighbors had a tractor and eight children so they could keep the open fields mowed, but my father worked in the city and traveled for his jobs, selling executive training programs or hearing aids or, one season, personalized matchbook covers. The grasses and short shrubs that had been left to flourish all summer were now so unruly they could only be burned to be contained.

The neighbor boy, David, and I had hiked down to the stream to check the dam. We had choked the neck of the flow with interwoven branches and rocks, easily quelling what was left of the drying trickle. It was getting harder and harder to find salamanders with the mud caking along the banks of what was usually replenished with a gush of water from under the big rock. We climbed up onto the rock and used our arrowheads to delicately scratch into our shins the symbols for friendship and long life. How easily the white welts healed before the smarting stopped. We possessed the hundred tests of Indian bravery, some of which we had yet to pass. These were the days of their devising and our arduous proofs: twenty drops of boiling water from a medicine dropper on our foreheads, biting into a live grasshopper. The escape from the other's hard-tied knots. The breaking of the hieroglyphic code. David could hold his breath longer, but I could stand the dark long after he would go inside at night.

What we heard first that day was a sharp crack in the upper registers of the trees, like a rifle going off. We raced up the hill from the streambed too late. What little wind there was had swept the fire in a path toward the woods, and we could see it shimmying all the way up the dry bark of the tallest trees. Where was my father?

Shielding my eyes from the smoke, I howled FIRE! and my next thought, rushing at the bedlam, panicked, rabbits shooting out from the heat into the still green grass, was *Now my life is beginning.* Forked orange in the owl's nest, orange-with-blue-breath in our maple-sugar house, orange fiends from our hidden forts forced up along with what the animals had—hunger, stealth, the grace of swift dispersal. David was keeping up with me. I yelled my insides out against the fire. *Daddy! Daddy! Get someone to help us!*

Faintly, the town alarm was summoning the volunteers. My father had gone inside to get a drink and the phone had rung. It took just that long, the steel rake leaning against the back door, his vigilance slack. And now the gulp and hurry of the fire, the high-boiled crackle of catching leaves and limbs. The volunteers coming so small and frantic in their pickups and canvas coveralls. With the truck's hose we filled the tanks and helped hoist them onto the men's backs. I dragged the hose as far toward the woods as it could possibly stretch. How strange, my father meaning to help, domestic, was suddenly this destroyer.

Until what we could not slake we fed. All throat and gray coughing gills, the fire's raw, involuntary swallowing we glutted with trees trees trees, refusing it nothing, felling a clearing wide enough to delay the fire with its own indulgence. Still not a single cloud of witness. The firemen staggered out of the heat for breath, their eyebrows and nose hairs singed. I had a cool cloth ready for their faces.

It took all day and into the night. My mother stayed inside the house with the other children and came out with sandwiches, I imagine, shielding her eyes with one hand, though I don't see her anywhere in my memory of the fire after she saw us running up the hill and called out the door to me, "Should I call the fire department?" The neighbors stood by the pump truck shaking their heads. There was nothing they could do but watch. An August brushfire unattended? The firemen surrounded the fire and with chain saws cut down the trees and vines most likely to catch and spread the blaze. Wetting the ground around the edges, they let the center of the worst fire they'd worked all summer burn. It could have spread for acres across the swamp, into the neighbors' barns. We were to keep an eye on it and call if the fire jumped its moat. But I must have fallen asleep, because my dream of the fire in our curtains jolted me to the window, where I leaned the rest of the night, watching. Let the moon think I did it, not my father. I could see the charred black trunks of the maples that would not revive. How long would it take for the lesser sumac and chokecherry, the honeysuckle to come back?

From where I stood, I could begin to see how different it would all be now, living here beside a ruined woods. My father wasn't one bit sorry about starting the fire. Oh, he might have been at first. When the fire looked like his only enemy he might have felt strong enough. He started to attack it on his own before the others got there with the right equipment. But it kept getting bigger and hotter, and when the volunteers showed up without saying anything, they let him know that they wouldn't have let this happen, ever, not them. So quietly, to himself, since they had set the standards of not saying things out loud, he had to defend himself to himself. He had to spread his anger at the fire around. Defenses up, it was hard to feel as regretful as he might have liked. When did what he did go wrong, anyway? It was perfectly acceptable to burn fields in the late summer. We saw field fires on every back road in the county this time of year. His rake was there, and the hose was coiled up beside the house a few yards away if he needed to turn it on. It is reasonable for a man to answer the phone. They were the ones being unreasonable. Accidents happen. Consider the percentages: this one happened this way, to him, but the next time it could just as well be them.

Not to them—but I wish he might have had the chance to say to me, early in the day, when the fire had just started into the edge of the woods, before he was too tired of fighting to forget, I wish he would have said, "How I regret starting that fire," or, "I was careless, are you all right?" He could have meant it. But by the time he fell asleep, he was actually almost glad he had started that fire. No average man would have risked what he had. Others couldn't see the profit, the drama of extremity the way he could. *This* was one memorable event, you know, and weren't they few and far between?

Of course I never had the chance to talk to him about the woods. He wouldn't have known about the scarlet Indian gum tendrils burning while the owl's nest simmered in the hollow trunk. The jack-in-the-pulpits were lost, and the trillium, the unbreakably thick half-plates of fungus, the vine-hung deer shelters, the squirrels' stash of seeds, the sap buckets the Amish boys had hung on the trees, the stream itself. Not moved, his regret was barely alerted before its cries were drowned out by the mere announcement, FIRE! His was a quick-shunted anguish. What couldn't he easily lose? What that was ours wouldn't he give away?

5 / *I*n my dictionary under "Estivation" are listed twenty types of prefloration, each with a compelling name and a small inky diagram. These are the varieties of ways a plant infolds within the bud, the ways the plant will show itself at the time of its blossoming. There are pinwheels and concentric rings, Ionic pods and nests of opposed scales. I wonder if the list is exhaustive or if, like the elements of the periodic table, the patterns of the hidden life of plants are still being discovered. Each sign is an allegory of waiting. Each figure exemplifies an ongoing preparation.

Think of enacting each of the patterns with your fingers; you need both hands, the enveloping, the curling like

the several ways a fetus lies cocooned and tucked within
the womb, almost ready. I am thinking of the patterns as
the many designs of first love, first kiss, first sex, and the
many other flabbergasting beginnings I (unremittingly) try
keep trying TRY to repeat, again. If a young girl's father
pays her even a minute's notice, lifts her one time onto his
shoulders so she can almost reach the fruit on the gnarled
tree, he is that first love. He becomes the template along
which the constructs of desire trace and are retraced. His
is the proportion of God, hers these intricate foldings and
unfoldings according to the pattern: involute, revolute, in-
duplicate, valvate, equitant, circinate, twisted, quincunx,
cochlear, curvative. There are more.

In the photograph he is my groom. We are smiling at
my mother, though my face is covered with a white net. I
am six; he has a flat blond crew cut. I have long blond
braids and a cocked smile. My nose, which has too wide a
bridge for me to have been a beautiful child, flares slightly
at the tip. I was pretending he was a distant cousin, having
heard from the girl across the street of the blood-relation
matrimonial taboos. Our children's heads would be so large
they would not fit on a pillow. They would be unmarriage-
able. Her father would not play along. He was married to
her mother. She would have to find her own true love. But
my father, until he grew so ill we had to lift him from his
bed, posed for my wedding pictures as a ringmaster, or a
thoughtful gardener. The gardener does not design the patterns but he cultivates them. The ringmaster does not tame
the tigers that pace their ornate gold-barred wagons.

Now I am eleven as the sun sifts through the trees in
glimpses. Light has a shadow self, a presence in water as

dusty beads strewn around us, displaced. It is the evening
of my baptism. In the shallow end of the neighbors' pool
my borrowed raincoat clings like the shroud I mean it to
be: to die in the span of one held breath. Sown in weakness,
raised in power. That first year of babysitting for the salesman's children I could not help slipping his magazines inside my notebook. To lift slightly off my haunches, hands
locked behind my head, to twist to see them watching my
back arch, my mouth shaped like the women's on the glossy
pages into O's, now licking our fingers, now barely touching
the tip of my tongue to my top teeth. The men must want
us to stroke ourselves. I do. I am the bride of Christ. Sown
in dishonor, raised in glory. As I lie back in the preacher's
arms, dusk's late warmth releases unevenly in the air. I let
him press me under, his trouser's full legs washing up at
his ankles, his jacket tails a wake. *In the name of the Father*,
I hear, and then inside the Spirit-of-Jesus cold I close my
eyes. We are virgins, our chastity a consummation. The
waters are enchanted; everyone is watching. His hands are
covering my mouth and nose. It is not mine to dispute; he
can feel my body rising with the water's muscle against
gravity or toward it.

My mother and her best friend wrapped me in a warm
towel. I had been quizzed on doctrine and had recited the
Scripture from memory. There was a lot of me to put to
rest and a lot of Christ to rise in me. I identified with Jesus,
three days in the tomb and then because of His perfection
resurrected. I identified with the Church, His spotless Bride.
I wanted to make a public ceremony of my faith so that
others could help me not forget. Sitting on the roof, where
I read in the hot smell of shingles and out of range of my
mother's calls to chores, I had discovered in the book of

Revelation the story of the wedding feast. Some would marry, some would be guests. Some were not invited at all. I didn't want to take that chance.

In the salesman's bedroom closet, though, I risked it all. Behind his perfect rows of suits and the angled shelves of polished shoes he had built a bookcase with rows and rows of paperback smut. I would prop his children in front of the television, or wait until they went to bed—he and his wife stayed out late—and then, over the course of six weeks or so, I read all the way through *Naked Came the Stranger*. She would just show up and in ten minutes an impotent man was cured. There were all sorts of bursts and sighs and a general wetness wherever the Stranger went. She did not discriminate. She knew their names or didn't, or forgot her underwear, or almost made him drive the car into the ditch. I'm making up what I can't remember. It's been years. I read once somewhere that the book had been a sort of party game that a group of writers devised. Each chapter was a different writer's fantasy, which was a disappointment, probably because as I read I had pictured one man who had fathomed such vile beauty as this, and instead there was a confederacy, who could know how extensive, of men and women in the thrall of secrecy and the many faces of the stranger.

Inside me were these two chronic susceptibilities of body and spirit. By thirteen my interior landscape was overrun with their mutual contagion. We had moved from the country where I had been raised among the Amish people, quilting, canning, watching pigs butchered behind the barn and eating them for supper. The boy I loved I loved purely for his love of the maps of places he would never see. By a kerosene light he traced the rivers for me, transposing dry

ground into connective estuaries or canals with a small stick
he had whittled to a point. What he did not take into account
were the headstrong currents of his imaginary waters. North
or South he could navigate the interiors of continents, equa-
torial or polar, even the deserts, but for him there was no
culminating Ocean. We were Baptists. We could float away
someday. And now we were in Cleveland, with all our le-
galisms incongruous but intact. We were not allowed to
swim with members of the opposite sex. If we were women
we wore head coverings, no jewelry or makeup, and skirts
(in the age of the mini) to the middle of our knees. We had
broken ties with one small congregation and joined together with five families to form another. We did not dance.
TOTAL DEPRAVITY. We did not celebrate the holidays,
except Thanksgiving, because we were not pagan—
UNCONDITIONAL ELECTION—nor did we follow rituals
of pagan institution. Nor drink, nor smoke—LIMITED
ATONEMENT—nor frequent theaters, nor tolerate a child's
deviations. IRRESISTIBLE GRACE. At school I kept to
myself as much as possible, waiting for the weekends,
when I wouldn't have to answer for my anachronisms. I
could babysit. Maybe there would be a potluck supper—
PERSEVERANCE OF THE SAINTS—and Charlie O. would
come.

The Osbornes were our church's poor, whose care the
five families that met together several times a week for
worship or meals or teaching took turns shouldering. They
lived in Cleveland city proper, behind the art museum.
There was the mother and her six children, whose father
was presumed no good for having left them indigent. It was
their dogs that my father disliked feeding with the slim
allowance he afforded them. The dogs, the children joked,

were always pregnant at the same time as their mother. The
children smelled of animals as they piled into our station
wagon on the Sunday mornings when it was our turn to
pick them up. My father's antipathy extended from the dogs
to Charlie, the only son, whose high black boots and guitar
strapped over one shoulder, whose manly stature at eighteen exerted a pressure that my heart's walls could not
sustain. Charlie would not sing the hymns, but he held the
book for me and stroked the back of my hand, weaving his
fingers between mine while I sang out the alto line. He
didn't come to services more than a few times. His sister
was sick with lupus and I saw him at the hospital once. As
though he didn't remember me, he turned around when I
pushed open the door to his sister's room, and then turned
back without saying anything to look out the window onto
the parking lot. There was one flower in a beaded white
vase. Her wrists looked inflated, the blue veins of her hands
stretched taut beneath the translucent skin. She slept sitting
up and leaning over a little in her bed.

The year of my father's first grave illness I turned sixteen. We had moved back to the country, to a different
town. I drove on Sunday evenings to a new church, which
met in a synagogue and where the people were caught up
in love. The members did not shake hands but embraced
each other at the door. Brother, they called each other, and
Sister. The group had not yet settled into organizational
hierarchies or personal scandal. My brother and sisters began to ask me if they could come along, and gradually even
our parents grew overburdened with the old rules. As a
family we began to celebrate holidays for the first time ever.
My father had given up hearing-aid sales for interior design.

It had been too difficult to convince the deaf of their need to hear. "They're paranoid that everyone is talking about them," he would say, "but they're too vain to put the tiniest battery in their ears." He had met someone and signed up for classes. He wanted to adapt his perfect eye for color, or his perfectly pitched ear to a profession more suited to his skills. So we moved to the town where his first design client had a weekend home. Dad was gone a lot for training. He had to check on progress at the drapery workrooms down-town, where he manned the design studio for his new partners.

Along the way he had met a man who gave him dozens of brightly colored striped and patterned shirts. Every week he would come home with more: short sleeves, red animal-patterned lace, a purple-and-white-striped silk that I begged him for.

"Why does he give you all these shirts?" my mother would ask him, giddy with that much generosity. "This beautiful pale blue linen!" though she didn't care as much for the loud prints. "He doesn't wear them anymore," my father told her. For most of that year my father lived in his bathrobe, once the hepatitis took control of his body. It was the bad lobster he had eaten. Yes, that was it.

"Shouldn't we tell the restaurant?" I asked. "Wouldn't their insurance help us?"

"I should look into that," he said, but knowing he had eaten no lobster, he never did. The doctor gave my parents the go-ahead on having sex. My mother kept a towel folded on the kitchen counter with his bottles of medication and a spoon and cup she sterilized with boiling water after feed-ing him. "Do you want me to go on reading?" she asked quietly, thinking he might have fallen asleep. His breathing was almost imperceptible. Even the automatic body functions taxed his weakness. His eyelids fluttered open, the skin the same stained yellow as the yellows of his eyes.

"Please," he whispered, and she read on. There were days he could walk in the yard, but mostly he lay sunk into the corner of the sofa in the living room, a sheet draped over the blue-and-white-flowered upholstery and over him. The sofa was pushed against the long wall with no windows; the light exhausted him. The younger children lived the best they could in a hush.

For my birthday, though, he insisted that my mother get him dressed. In a restaurant with sixteen classmates he pretended were my friends, he had arranged sixteen roses with a ten-dollar bill tied to each stem. I think the boy I went with to the prom was most impressed. The boy was silly, I knew, even then, and the roses seemed too lavish a display for the occasion. My father's effort would initiate a deepening collapse that drove my mother nearly to despair. She could not get him to drink the broth from his spoon. He must have borrowed the money, so I gave it back.

By then there was someone else who I imagined had given me the roses. I would sit in the third row of his Shakespeare class so that the other girls could not see me watch him—the place where his olive-skinned arm met the loose cloth of his T-shirt sleeve, the fade of his jeans, his long black hair like the lover's in the Song of Songs. He had participated in the Kent State riots and smoked pot with the seniors in his van. He was the sole faculty member who sided with the students on the issue of a smoking lounge, and rallied for free paint for the cafeteria walls. We were both left-handed. He carried his tall lean body like a cause, forward and sure, but with enough relaxed slowness that he had the appearance of already having won. In front of the whole class he would dance with our imaginations' spoils. Near the end of the period he would turn to me, after waiting all those minutes. Maybe it would be a question he had written on the board that only I could answer, or a paper he would hand back with comments in the margin like "droll" or "just so." His parents were Arabs, I thought I heard him tell someone. But I don't remember asking him. His past didn't involve me. What he believed about Hermann Hesse or Andrew Marvell or Carson McCullers did. And what he believed about what I thought but had never said aloud before: what kind of an artist I was, how did I know? The dialogue was taken up in the pages of the assignments I turned in, the thought-papers that registered more of me than of the books assigned, and that he seemed to treasure.

"Whatever you may think, it's beyond a crush," I wrote in my journal. "He loves ME too. It is how we will resist our love that will save us." The journal was his idea. For Christmas he had given me the red leather-bound Kahlil Gibran Diary for 1974, with selections from *The Prophet* introducing each week and Gibran's sensual drawings of beings part earthly, part spiritual scattered between the months. *The Seed: A pearl is a temple built by pain around a grain of sand. / What longing built our bodies and around what grains?* I addressed my thoughts on the journal's pages to an unspecified "You." In it I tried to record the accelerating rivalry of desires, one day pressing my mouth onto the page and writing over the marks of lips and breath, the next tearing the page into repentant shreds. I was a temple of the Holy Spirit. "I will win your soul to Christ. You will initiate me into your eternity I dream of and wake to the whole infant and ancient year I am sixteen." A quick breakfast, the bus a blur. He would arrive earlier than I could so we didn't have to wait.

In my journals—as in my life—there was the problem of what to call him. I knew his given name, of course, but having called him, along with all the other students, by his surname the year before, that name was how I thought of him. Which felt absurd. Didn't he call me Susan? So I didn't call him anything most of the time, or I called him Mister, as in, You'd better watch it, Mister, or, I love you, Mister. On the page he sometimes shows up by initial, or I have someone else refer to him. What he called discretion became my layered dishonesties. A show for them, a show for us. How we avoided speaking of his infidelity was to feature in our trysts as the problems of Time and Age. He was twenty-seven. I had another year of high school. We had fifteen minutes a day to be alone.

There are entries about student government and about art. I had drawn a series of self-portraits with multiple images on a single page. My face is looking both straight ahead and to the side, and I write about this: *Desire for Life: And when you were a silent word upon Life's quivering lips, I too was there, another silent word. Then Life uttered us and we came down the years throbbing with memories of yesterday and with longing for tomorrow, for yesterday was death conquered and tomorrow was birth pursued.* Between the lines, my conflicted desires rage from utterance to silence: there are always two of us about to speak.

The journal's central running theme is "the other sex," the incidence of encounter heightening the pitch of the diction until an entry either expires in a prayer of thanks

or is signed—as though the page itself were masculine—
"Love, Susan." There is an insistence in the writing, when
attraction flares, on what I refer to throughout as the "platonic." Platonic meant that both the male and the female
could "resist the physical" and interact by mutual agree-
ment in mental and spiritual harmony. My spirit was willing
but my flesh was not. She is confused in front of herself.
She turns away. On one page the grandiloquence of righteousness, on the next the flat bathos of a sixteen-year-old
girl's moondreams.

The way it started was that I had fallen off my bicycle
and crushed my mouth against the curb. One lip had split
open and the other was swollen. I held the back of my hand
up to my mouth when I opened the English office door.
The department chairman (my after-school tutor in the formal elements of poetry, the tests of rhythm, shape, meter,
caesura) rose to leave when I arrived, mumbling his excuses
of preparation, glancing back and meeting, I think, both of
our eyes for an instant before he closed the door behind
him.

My hand with the bitten fingernails in front of my face;
the hand he took and kissed in mock gallantry, not noticing
yet, and then, pulling me to him gently, he looked from my
mouth with the dried blood along the corner to my eyes. It
was not that this was the best tenderness of its kind—I had
nothing to compare it with—but that it was the first. "Don't
look at me," I said, turning my face away, and staying up
close to him. This was as far as I had envisioned. But he
had my head in his hands and was touching faintly around
the bruise and the cut lower lip with his tongue, like a dog,
I thought confusedly, the thought tossed up out of my awk-

wardness and longing. The severe tenderness soothed my mouth, though I couldn't let it.

The body flowering is greedy, and secretive; its pleasures hoard the mind, hoard guilt as though there were no help for its fecund devouring. The way the spirit grows is steady, too, once it begins, though its evolution is more difficult to recognize. You cannot make it happen by a volitional strike, suddenly. The visible bursts, the unseen foliates. The arrangement within the bud must loosen of its own accord.

I had a friend who walked with me along a spiritual path for a while. When Matthew came back from Princeton for the summer, we drove his jeep with the top off to go look for shoes for him. He had a size 14 foot, so narrow that nothing fit. Matthew was holy already, and the smell of him so strong I think the lake we swam in changed its fragrance when he dove in. He smelled like an African market, and eucalyptus, and tansy, and gasoline. Whatever else I was was over. We spent the summer between our houses and at his family's hunting lodge. We took our separate blankets out into the field at midnight and lay there until we could pick out the constellation we'd elected from the planisphere. It is because of those nights I can find the wide-mouthed W that is Cassiopeia, and Orion's studded belt—the summer stars that year after year in honor of the equinoxes return to their places right on time. Between us there was the impossibility of spoiling the ideal form of friendship; as if we were a model, not quite actual, we didn't dare touch. Though my father refused to believe it. Part of the energy he needed to recover trickled from him in allusions to the effect that I was lying to myself.

S U S A N   B E R G M A N   (84

But now I had nothing to hide. Matthew had apprenticed himself to a Greek Orthodox priest and was teaching the lives of the Eastern saints to me. His family was perplexed. All five of the handsome brothers had their talents and capacities, but none like his. It was not until the shortening days of that summer that he took his Orthodox name and left us all. We were encumbrances he had loved well but who he now believed could not partake in his ultimate spiritual quest. He came to the front door and knocked instead of the usual walk right in. I slid down the stairway railing from my bedroom when I saw his jeep pull into the drive all packed for where? His greeting was stiff, his head sitting back too far on his neck, so that as he looked from my gold-hoop earrings to my Danskin leotard I wore under a long print skirt I felt from him what seemed like condemnation. From someone else's monologue he intoned, "It is heaven I need to follow." I could see he had rehearsed. "I've come to see you last, to say goodbye." He was not pretending.

"You haven't told me anything about this!" I was startled. We hadn't been together for a week, maybe eight days, but "Where do you think you're going, Mister?" He was nothing like Mister, but I called him that as he stood by the door and wouldn't grab on when I reached for his hands. He was going to California, to the monastery where he would complete his Greek studies and prepare himself to help the Church Fathers with translation. "Is she beautiful?" I tried to joke, then stiffened at the awesomeness of the high calling I knew he would not betray. He had just a few minutes more to talk about his plans. Feebly I offered my regard for his dedication.

"There can be no help from you," he said, shaking his

head. "You are not part of the plan." I didn't deserve to
be, I knew, which made me cry a little.

"I'm going to miss you like crazy, then." Tomorrow, I
thought, he'll call, but no. Matthew belonged to the platonic
ranks of the five regular geometric solids. We could not
corrupt one another, being from separate orders, his min-
eral to my vegetable. That was how we had preserved the
decorum between us, and perhaps why he still will not
answer my letters.

It was near closing time at the end of the summer, after
Matthew had already gone away, that I saw the familiar
van pull into the garden center where I worked. The flowering plants in the front rooms had all been watered, the
metal picks attached to the artificial flowers Mrs. Hisset
would arrange in imitation of the Teleflora photograph.
She saw him coming in the front door and quickly smeared
on the coral-colored lipstick she reapplied in front of the
tiny office mirror for her best customers. He told her he
was going to need a little time to look around, for a gift,
not seeing me at first; then, as Mrs. Hisset answered the
phone, he ducked out the front door, pulling me after him
into the fading summer evening.

"We're going for a ride," he said, sliding back the door
of his van. He had driven me places before. Inside was like
the inside of a genie's lair, with carpets and the blended
aromas of patchouli and reckless smokes. All this time I
hadn't thought of school, or him, and now his friend, my
history teacher—the one with the acne scars and the sense
of the world as a grand sports metaphor—was sitting in the
front passenger seat.

"Mr. Buttleman," I said, surprised.

"Make it Dave." He nodded, blearily. He too had been corrupted, I understood, his pot-face blurring into a flatter and flatter smile with the new sensation of his high. I breathed in the heavy spice of the closed space, not wanting to see my whole set of saints, and my devotion, spinning into orbit right then. Why were we stopping on a country road not far from my house? Mister opened the back door again and I hopped out. It was time for me to be home for dinner. I hadn't said goodbye to anyone at work.

"Why is *he* here?" I asked, tossing my head in the direction of the front window. In my mind our secret was completely hidden from view. I would get passes out of chemistry lab if I finished early because that was his free period. Or we would stagger our escapes out to the woods behind the school if the coast was clear. He would wrap the deep red velvet curtains backstage in the school audi-torium around us until we were just another prop. But to my mind our attraction had been invisible. There was no place for it in the world, and so for the world it did not exist. He had covered with a friendliness, a light touch, or a considerate length of after-school contact with several other students we both knew. I sneaked into the band prac-tice rooms when no one was watching and waited for him there, playing Gershwin and Judy Collins on the piano, or practicing my scales. "Do you know what I want you to do?" he would ask me when I was far enough under the spell of his mesmerism to comply. Or was it my malign charm? Ours had been an unspoken complicity; now he was breaking open the secret without having offered me the choice.

"What, are you afraid Dave's going to tell your mother?" he asked, derision in his voice. A car threw up dust and gravel behind it on the road. Out in the coming dark the rows of corn, the crickets turning on, with his friend pretending to keep busy in the front seat, I couldn't think of anything to say. He wasn't my teacher anymore. He must have fought with his wife. He didn't even have the pretense of a desk or books or a lesson plan. Whenever I walked down the hallways I had been superior somehow, I was his favorite, but after a summer apart I envied my friend who had a boyfriend her own age whom she might marry. My body wouldn't come on. I leaned on him with my back and shoulders against his chest, not wanting to feel his erection.

"Do you ever get jealous?" I asked, to mute the silence.

"Of what?" He was pulling my blouse tail out of my shorts.

"Of who else I will love?" I tucked my shirt back in.

"No, I don't." He was sure without having to think about his answer.

His only rival for my heart was God, who seemed pale and helpless next to this vivid man. I turned around into him, my arms bent in front of me like a soft shield, and leaned my face into his shoulder. He wrapped me up in him until he felt me release my future, my history, my father's illness, and what would be my mother's horror to see me in my teacher's arms. I could feel his cheek stroking my face up toward his. They were almost black eyes.

"I'm moving out West," he whispered, like a part of my own body speaking. It was already August. We had three weeks.

My father moved slowly, stiff-limbed after his long confinement; like a wobbly just-born animal trying out its legs, his body would alternately gain strength and collapse.

When he grew strong enough to eat at the table, we burned his snagged blue bathrobe. We could not wash the sickness out of it or look at it limp on the back of the bathroom door for one more day. The summer was ending with promise. A halting resuscitation in our household stirred us all to plans. It would be my last year at home. My father would be well again.

Maybe I would still adore my teacher—I keep wanting to say *she* would adore *her* teacher. I still dream about him. He comes back. When he sees me he hesitates for a moment, making sure nobody is watching us, then he motions for me to follow him into a room with no windows and, once we're inside, no doors. I was drunk on his fondling, but more so on his gifts of books and ideas. I am trying to cultivate that early passion without sneaking off to a father surrogate. Let me try again.

The way it started was, after school one day he was sitting on top of a teacher's desk in an empty classroom and we were talking about Howard Roark and Dominique from Ayn Rand's *Fountainhead*. Roark was an architect who could, for principle's sake, explode the very building he had designed. Dominique could slash her neck and arms until she fell unconscious, to disguise her love for a man. I was sitting in front of him and stood up suddenly, overcome with the characters' pure sufficiency. In one passage she is lying on a wide bed upstairs, the whole plot conspiring to have Roark open the door and want her. But he leaves before they make love, I think before they even touch, and the whole book quivers with the strength of his self-denial.

Or I quivered, and standing up, I took the two or three steps to him and straddled his one knee so that my thighs

surrounded and moved along his thighs. I just did it, as-
tonishing myself and him. He had to grab me around the
waist or I would have lost my balance. Beyond that he didn't
respond by touching me, only by trying to look in further
to what I must be thinking. I stared back hard.

"Lady"—he left a long pause hanging—"do you know
what you're doing?" he asked.

It was not my parents' rules, or the school's, or the
Bible's I was transgressing so much as my own developing
spirit. I wanted to take in all experience that could teach
me without destroying the light. But when I touched him,
at the same moment that my body pulsed on, the light inside
me flickered. I was all there, wholly present. I would have
to divide into parts and put one outside and the other over
there. The parts would be wrapped in separate colored papers. I would open them up when I was ready. The mind
begins to legislate. The body craves equal time. The spirit
rises to sing and is placed far away, under something that
will muffle it. And the clamor of conflicting passions sounds
outlying passions like a gong. I stepped back and ran from
the room.

The way it started—however far back I can go along
the avenue of a glance (she knows that he is watching her
and she is watching him), beyond the compelling drive,
back to nurture, and lack of nurture, into the genetic codes
of addiction and overwhelming need—the way it started,
the prescient start, like a first principle, encodes its end in
its embryo.

I had just finished my period. I was dry. He was moving
to Colorado, so I went to see him for the last time at his
apartment. I had been there before on his enormous wa-

terbed, but I would leave my clothes on as we touched, lightly, more like wrestling. Once, I wore my favorite caramel-colored lamb's-wool sweater with the tiny moth hole at the neck. What he liked best was the feel of me in my father's purple-and-white-striped silk shirt without a bra. When I got there this time, he didn't want me to go into his apartment, so I stood outside in the hallway waiting for him to finish whatever it was he had to do and then lock the door. He was all packed to move, or his wife might come home, but he had a key for an empty apartment down the hall with a few pieces of inexpensive furniture including, in a single back bedroom, one twin bed without any sheets.

Usually we had music. There were the remains of the last tenant's plants on the windowsills, dead from heat and neglect. August's trill of heat. The walls were thick with overpainting; in this incarnation they were what would have normally been a forgettable mustard gold. I must have been wearing a skirt. I had brought my journal to let him read the last few pages. They were poems about him now that he was going away, and about me. I would shelter the light from the wind of our desire now. They were a girl's poems, troubled with the drifts of sex and faith and words. When he finished reading them he read a few lines out loud to me, with sonorous deliberation, as though they had been written by an ancient bard. As he read them I sat on the arm of the sofa with my feet in his lap, his arm draped over my knees.

"These are by far your best," he told me. "You are right here in the words, and the words are transparent."

To desire virtue, I pretended not to notice, is its own form of seduction. I admitted the magnetisms of a game of chess, how the opening moves lock you and your opponent into moats of dependency. I knew the maddening itch that being ignored aroused, but not that purity is a dare.

His fingers followed along the front of my thighs and hooked under the elastic of my panties. I had resolved not to, and chosen my oldest cotton pair. He helped me stand up on the couch and step out of them. They fell off like a useless skin which he picked up to smell. At the same moment that he reached for me, I let my legs swing around his hips, so he could carry me to the other room. We were going to, without music, at the callow end of the interminable summer of my abandonment.

He took his penis out of his pants and rubbed against me, on my belly, high up between my legs; I tried to help him, on the dry folds of my labia. This was going all wrong. There was no time to unwrap the right elements so that even one part of myself could be included, could begin its justifications to the others. Yet I couldn't help this sense of being an accomplice. He pushed in and I felt his zipper cut into my skin as he rocked two or three times and as abruptly pulled out. As if he had been thrown from me, he reared back and fell against the wall.

"There was no way I was going to let that happen," he moans, shaking. I finish buckling his belt for him. I draw him back down to the bed and make him lie on his back so I can lie along the whole length of him. There is a song I am humming before I think of what the words are, and when I think of the words I stop. It is I who am no good at ending. That was it, wasn't it? Was that it? I smooth his hair away from where it has stuck to the sweat on his neck, and he shudders. I have to drive home fast and get into the shower.

The blasting heat a farewell, the shock of walking on

the way to my car past people who will forget this day's significance. The green lights a farewell. Go on, go on. The woman placing a pale envelope into the mailbox. The white lines of the road interrupted, but going on, and beyond the place where I turn off onto the gravel roads that will take me to my road, the white lines continuing.

We are as seen from life, an artifice,
an emphasis, an uncompleted arc perhaps.
—Y E A T S , *Autobiography*

6   /   *M*y father clipped the notice from a local paper: "Talent search! Singers, dancers, magicians wanted. Top-paying summer positions in the Fabulous Fifties Musical Review at Geauga Lake Amusement Park, Aurora, Ohio. Open auditions May 7." He placed the scissors back in the divider alongside the paring knife and the melon baller, renesting the serving spoons inside the slotted spoons before closing the drawer. This job would surely hold more appeal than most for a girl Susan's age. Is that what he believed, that I would like it, that it would be good for me? He presented the possibility at dinner.

School would be out in a month and I was trying to

line up a job as a counselor at a Salvation Army camp. Or Mrs. Hisset would always take me back at the Garden Gate, where I could help customers choose perennials to fill in their flower borders. Flowers for personalities: the prissy, multichambered columbine and the Jackmanii clematis with its overeager growth for Victorian ladies, and the uncommon cimicifuga and alstroemeria I kept from all but those whose lives I imagined to be rare. But I liked to perform, and my father liked the idea of my being close to home the last summer before I'd go to college. "Only if you want to," he said. I thought I knew what he wanted. "We could work up a number this weekend. You've got a few days to decide."

He accompanied me on all my auditions for school musicals and community theater productions. Local directors knew they could call on him to fill in on the piano for rehearsals or performances if the orchestra didn't work out, and partly for this reason, partly because he rehearsed me so well for my roles, I was always cast as the character I had set my heart on. Earlier that year I played the part of the youngest daughter, Chava, in *Fiddler on the Roof*, and later Juliet in Kent State University's Shakespeare in the Park. I was Cecily Cardew in *The Importance of Being Earnest*, and Sylvia in *Up the Down Staircase*. But by the end of my senior year I had pretty well decided to pursue painting and leave acting and piano to those whose strength was interpretation. What would a vaudeville review at an amusement park contribute to my future? But then, what was a camp in the mountains, or the privilege of flowers? How could trying hurt? I would give it a shot.

I spread the music on the piano for my father to play, counting out the measures of introduction the first time through without coming in. I wanted to hear the whole song as he would arrange it, his fingers light across the octaves until he worked back to the beginning, where he nodded for me to begin. Keeping the rhythm with my shoulders I tried, *Oh, listen, sister, / I love my mister man, / And I can't tell yo' why*. Already I was straining instead of breathing; my voice sounded small and hollow. "Let's work on phrasing first," my father suggested, and he interpreted the first few lines himself, singing much more easily in sync with his own playing. I mimicked his inflection, took a breath from my lower belly: *Dere ain't no reason / Why I should love dat man*. The word "man" slurred a little, but not with the sureness I wanted to end with.

"What about singing 'there,' instead of 'dere'?" I said. "I'd feel less phony." We tried it that way, but what to do with *It mus' be sumpim' dat de angels done plan*? I went back to the idiom as written. We worked on the song late into the night, my mother putting the younger children to bed and glancing into the room from time to time with a smile of encouragement.

I tried to picture the way Dionne Warwick would sing the song, or Carmen McRae. They would get the part and I wouldn't. The competition wouldn't be that stiff; there was still time to back out.

It was a Sunday afternoon when we drove through the entrance gate at the old amusement park and made our way to the line of cars already in the parking lot. The park was scheduled to open on Memorial Day, which gave us less than three weeks to rehearse. On the fairway mechanics were tightening bolts and reinforcing girders on the rickety Big Dipper. Men dangling on ropes with paint cans hooked to their belts retouched the white wooden mesh of the old roller coaster's scaffolding. They replaced the double strand of lights on the Yo-Yo swings. I was more nervous than usual, thinking of being paid to do what I had always volunteered to have a part in. My father, adamant as ever, insisted that the part was mine if I wanted it.

Inside the theater the auditions had begun. Hundreds of people stretched in the aisles limbering up for their turn under the lights, or lounged against the walls reading magazines, or propped themselves conspicuously on the backs of velvet chairs. They would need five women and five men. We were to sing a song of our own choosing and part of a song from the show—to the tune of "That's Entertainment," with new words. Everyone in the theater, as if according to some master cue I had failed to heed, had made themselves up for the stage with heavy lines drawn around their lips and eyes. No one appeared to be under twenty. Where were all the high-school students I had expected to see? Had the notice said anything about a minimum age? My long, straight hair was parted down the middle and tucked behind my ears. I combed my fingers through it to coax a little volume.

At the upright piano onstage a man with a few tufts of hair above each ear, wearing a T-shirt and dangling an unlit cigarette from the corner of his mouth, was running through a number by sight for the woman who was about to sing. They seemed to know each other already. She fed him the time by slowing down her hips until he played the song at the tempo she beat with her eyes closed. Dazzling him, so confident, she leaned over the edge of the stage toward the show's director with a question or a joke, touching him playfully on the cheek, so that they both threw their heads back laughing as she took her place in the center of his attention. "From the top, please." Only on Broadway had I seen someone this right for show biz, this at home. She had chosen a song perfectly suited to her voice's low range and let her body effortlessly captivate both her competition and the judges. "Dynamite, Jeannie," the director called out before she had let go all the way of her last husky note. "I think we know what you can do. Get changed for the dance number." The room erupted in applause and whistles.

A thin, unhealthy-looking man with deep circles around his eyes took the steps two at a time to try his luck. One foot caught in his bell-bottom trousers and he nearly lost his balance. In and out, in and out he labored to breathe, trying to relax himself, but couldn't. The quaver in his voice he managed to submerge just below the surface through the first verse of a song he himself had composed, but at the chorus a tremulous wail suddenly broke through his unintelligible lyrics and became a sort of piercing scat. He tried to bolster the phrase but lost his wind, and the director's voice boomed out an octave lower, "A be-biddy-op-shoowop." The man stopped holding his body so stiffly, as if relieved to have someone else take over for him. His hands fell by his side and dangled there, too heavy for his arms, while the director thanked him for his time in a stage whisper we all heard. The man excused himself to the air in the room and gathered his things before leaving.

There would be a break, and when we came back it would be my turn. They had bungled the pronunciation of my name when they called it; so what! I found the bathroom and stood in front of the mirror with seven or eight women who were applying another layer of makeup, pulling out lipstick tubes and compacts, brushes and sprays that smelled in the tension of close air like the powdery aroma of a place I had read about in a book. In the light flaring on the mirror's surface, my face gaped entirely plain and uneventful. Next to all the other women's color I could barely see my own mouth. My smile looked worried or stunned, acquired, not genuine. Where were my eyes?

"Are you kidding me?" my father said as I told him how worried I was that I wasn't quite what they were looking for. "Those women spend hours a day trying to make themselves look like you." There it was—his seemingly random standard and the perfect match he'd sired to meet it. "Now sing like I know you can."

It was my father's openhanded praise of me as a girl, however crimped my resources or capabilities, fused with his majestic expectations, as though my life were invaluable and urgent, that informed my sense of place in the world. If the whole room were peopled with dancers costumed and ablaze, should the Queen propose tea, were I to believe it possible to win whatever race, whatever contest . . . dream on, dream your arms and head thrown back, first across the finish line, the flag at the mountaintop, the car wheels hot with victory, a beauty's crown, the Queen so courteous, the dancers whirling their congratulations, rise above them.

Whether it was groundless or due to wishful thinking, my parents inflated their children's sense of capability, which buoyed us through childhood and became a habit difficult to sink. They were enhancing, with no sense of the ceilings on possibility, the ordinary lives their parents had entrusted to them. The best, quickest, smartest, most extraordinary; my mother would copy, with minor variations, the list she had by heart onto all our birthday cards and in later years our Christmas stocking notes from Santa. Believing them (they were our parents), we were kept busy filling the many chambers of their hopes. To think of the moon as one's personal luminance, its rotations, waxings, and wanings within reach—we believed because we didn't yet know otherwise. We recognized the hype (Daddy will get it for you) one telling incident at a time.

So the mixed curse and blessing of our unfounded sense of merit began to unfold. We would have to trade in honest work for others' allowances. What was once incomprehensible, that those who saw us—as those who didn't —went on with their lives in utter indifference to our postures and flauntings, we now more easily take for granted.

The degree of incapacitation (waking from the fantasy) has varied among us. Because of the wide spread of years from me to my brother and sisters—I was eight when the first of them was born—we experienced different stages of disillusionment. I was fathered by a young man just into his twenties, full of potentialities and energies that enabled his promises and dreams, more often than not, to come true. While I had met the sheriff at the door, giving him the keys to the Cadillac the dealer was repossessing, by the time Anne drank from the mirage, it was more evidently dry.

In 1975 the family had moved from Ohio to the Jersey shore. There was a season of seeming prosperity while my father depleted the investors' capital for his new venture. But quickly the oil-drilling scheme went bust. Anne had listened to the scrape of her brother's and sister's spoons on the bottom of a bowl of watered-down soup. That dinner made them cross with each other after several nights. And yet the aging would-be/could-be was talking and walking big. Atlantic City suited him.

I still harbor a dreamer's vision of my potential. More rarely now, I entertain notions of grandeur, daring to rush in, only to disappoint myself. My father's high hopes worked for me as a child, but the slope keeps steepening. No one warned us. Nathan raced with his lights off, practicing invincibility, until he died. Abigail struts her mortality, bent today on almost staying alive. Anne's forced drive works to outpace her own dreams, which she shrinks from, working. Working is what it takes, not talking about it. She gets the role in the film for trying hard and because she's good. She runs into the studio for a costume fitting and her leading man is there waiting to try on his clothes. She knew he'd been cast, but hadn't expected to see him yet.

"He actually got up from his chair and came over and gave me a hug! Can you believe it? Him hugging me!"

"Why not?" I ask her.

"Why not? Because I'm Anne Heche, nobody. He doesn't even know I exist. And he's the first real actor I ever admired."

Anne and I had been talking about this disparity between us in the wake of our father's illusions. How the two of us are doing what we want to do from seemingly opposite ends of motivation's scale—one from the habit of dreaming, the other to escape the dream's snagging power. Feigned merit, a sense of unworthiness, both sides work from defenses we would like to shed. The latter says "HE hugged me?" and the former says, "Mister! it's about time."

I can see it now reflected on the surface of my own ornate shield—the gilded cant that passed for reality in my

family, the rave reviews we passed among ourselves re-
porting on others' admiration. The world was jealous, my
father told us, of our lives. We would be persecuted for our
excellence. If we peered through the filter of our father's
lens, he was a family man, joined in glorious marriage,
pride of my mother, who was his pride. We could see the
envious scan us, up and down, from our blond hair and
blue eyes to our cuffed socks and polished shoes. We
watched them green around the gills. We could not sit on
the beach or walk on the boardwalk without being interrupted by someone wanting to partake in the family per-
fectability they could see we shared, one man going so far
as to approach with his camera. Could he take our picture?
Would we mind terribly?

In the spirit of appearance my father had once quit his
job selling hearing aids or insurance, taken me out of
school, and packed us off to Indiana (my mother only mildly
protesting), to care for his dying father, whom he despised,
and mind the family's backwater grocery, which his mother
struggled with alone. As a boy he had intercepted the flail-
ing blows and oaths meant for her, placing his body in the
gap between them. He had thrashed through whole nights,
overhearing beneath the floorboards the furniture being
shoved or thrown, the tear of cloth, a mirror broken, and
much later a weak man's whimper of remorse.

At the walk-in cooler of his parents' grocery store my
father opened the heavy wooden door and disappeared inside to find the slab of bacon and the orange round of Colby
cheese. His customer wanted them sliced just so: the bacon
this thick, her fingers shaping the width pudgily in air, and
the cheese like a thin sheet of salty wax. That was how I

liked the cheese, so I waited for my father by the electric slicer. If I held my mouth open like a little bird, he would feed a rolled-up slice onto my tongue and it would melt almost before I could taste it.

I was nine that year. My grandfather's lungs and liver, his heart—in my child's mind I thought of him as a heap of flaking, blackened parts—was dying and we were there to help, for as long as we were needed. My grandmother was grateful for her son's devotion. He would drive her to and from the hospital, trying not to hate her, too, her limitations and self-pity. It was his own ideal image of filial provision he was living out, not hers; she hadn't the imagination or the self-regard to impose one.

This must be how honor looks—he was at the fitting, trying his costume on—to leave your job in order to care for your dying parent, comforting the survivors, setting the example. To place the weekly orders for the cereals and baked goods, the canned vegetables and fruits, the fresh produce and meats. To arrange and replenish shelves. To sweep the oiled wooden floors, balance the ledgers, freshen the bait, pump the gas; to fulfill one's parents' unuttered demands. His would be his children's standard—a child such as he was, devoted and ever exceeding his parents' wildest rhapsodies—wrapping the cheese and bacon in white butcher paper and tying it with a string. It was his conscience that would bother us.

We had my father's standards to uphold. Not a word to others about money or private family business. Silence on matters of discipline and affection. Though, like a trickle from a crumbling dam, facts leaked out. My father had been fired from his job. His timely devotion shored up the wall of his seeming. What might others say? What did others have to do with us? As we thought back, more often than we had the capacity to acknowledge, we must have been pitied by those whose lives consisted of substance and not show, pitied or scorned, though we remained oblivious to disdain. People were looking. We were on view. This indiscriminate worry we directed toward the woman at the checkout counter, strangers leaning out of cars, the pastor, church members whose greeting failed to conceal our shared but inadmissible family crazing, but who admired —yes, they did—our flawless glaze. Not secrets, children, but discretion.

Our father had in mind the staging of a family drama that our mother's complicity propped up. Just like the photographs: every hair in place, our coordinated clothes, show your teeth when you smile, she liked life that way. And for this I am apt to defend my father to my mother, like a case worker before the courts. Like a bulletproof vest shielding against some hypothetical assailant. Sometimes my defense is inadvertent, sometimes taunting, like a spider dangling near my mother's face. One day I spun out a strand of thought and hung there on the other end of the telephone line, just out of reach.

"What if Daddy had come home and announced once and for all, had said out loud, 'Honey' (that's what he called my mother), 'I've got AIDS—got it from one of my male lovers. You don't know him; I didn't mean to.'" To my mother his confession is unimaginable. She is thinking about this now, the idea of his admission being more revolting and out of character than his betrayal. She would have had to . . . (unthinkable). How could she have faced her life without her marriage, which was all she ever wanted, and children?

"You're right, of course. I'd never even thought of that scenario." She was grateful to have had pointed out to her this alternative to the life she'd lived, the secrecy, the window dressing. What she got was what she wanted. It was better this way. The props worked.

I wasn't implying that fraudulence and hypocrisy were better. That was, in fact, the opposite of what I'd meant to suggest. I had wanted to commiserate with the duped that day, having felt since I woke up my own plumbless gullibility. I'd wanted to bemoan the years he'd pretended and we'd all played along—to undo those years, or redo them with a naked eye. The better to see you with. But my mother had converted my regrets over a life of pretense and theatrics into the prospect of her own relief. She had momentarily considered the alternative and deemed her lot the lesser ill, now that I mentioned it. That is my mother's way: to wring out survival from various rocks. Think only the best thoughts. She was at work and needed to meet with a client in a few minutes to review their investment strategy. "I'm so glad you called, sweetie, you've given me a lot to be grateful for."

We hung up the telephone. It would be a long day, so that by tenish, a bluesy, strung-out jazz on the radio, the seesaw of contempt and devotion pivoting on my ambivalence—what if there were no point of balance to be achieved concerning one's feelings about one's father?—would thunk down hard on the ground. Liar, thief of one's birthright. Isn't a child entitled to be fathered by a man who loves women, if not one's mother, for life? I couldn't think of anyone I knew for whom this pure mother love was the uninterrupted case (though I didn't know anyone else with a father who loved men). All the accomplice mothers, I count them on my fingers. What alternatives did they have to the choices they'd made? I hate this kind of soft-headed sympathy: She couldn't help it. It's the reason my mother recovers more quickly than I do. She cares for others, disregarding her out-of-pocket costs. "Poor thing," she says. She dates now and looks better than ever.

My mother moves on and I sit here reshuffling scenes and acts, stack the new information I've been gathering next to familiar facts. Houselights, please, let's take it from the top. I get in position for the number called "Regret," which I have by heart. Rerun one dialogue back over another. There must be something to savor in my parents' gift—what continued in me of their dauntlessness, what had not been corrupted by my own skepticism and counterbalancing. They loved me to death. The backswing of blind confidence is disablement: from a blitzing stride to flimsy step. I could waft from a room.

People were regathering near the front of the stage. The select few who had been designated for the next round sat in the row of chairs behind the director, talking loudly and laughing. They were caught up in a sort of rapture. I would be left behind, stopped dead in my tracks, only to watch them rise into the clouds. My father had gone to speak with the tuft-haired man at the piano, who seemed reluctant to give up his post onstage. The man flicked his ash into his hand and shrugged toward the director, who waved him over to consult with him briefly before nodding to my father, who was already sitting down to play the chords and runs he used to get acquainted with a foreign keyboard.

I had never practiced with a microphone. It sputtered as I tried to disconnect it from its stand. How close or far from my face should I hold the thing? It could hear me breathing. I could blow into the whole room's ear. The director was still talking with the choreographer about the way my legs looked, I supposed, too thin and a little bowed. Should I start anyway? I looked over at my father, who raised both eyebrows: Was I ready? The words . . . *Fish gotta swim and birds* . . . No, it starts out . . . that's the chorus. His introduction played twice rescued me.

Not sultry, not glib, I needed just the right image of a man I couldn't help loving for the mood I was trying to summon. In the whole room there was only my father who sparked any feeling whatsoever other than trepidation. He was smiling at me, proud, and I was thinking of the words as they came one after the other with the tune and the tempo good and slow: *It mus' be sumpin' dat de angels done plan.* Then the piano interlude before I started the second verse. I had too much time to think of other songs I would rather have been singing. I was doing this for my father; what did he want out of my life? Only last year he wouldn't have let me see the show or attend my school dances, and here I was slinging my way through a love song, needing to appear intrepid in a black woman's voice I had no skill for.

Time. I started humming until the words came: *hmmmmmm—De chimbley's smokin', / De roof is leakin' in, / But he don' seem to care.* My father was mouthing the words exaggeratedly. We were almost finished now. *When he goes away-ay, / Dat's a rainy day-ay/* . . . At the time I must have felt that distraction was called for, or emphasis, so I started doing something with my hands in front of everybody that I hadn't tried at home, adding in little illustrative gestures for each line, raindrops, a sip of gin, an outline of a smile, with both hands lifting along the corners of my mouth for *he can be happy*. Even as I moved I felt the absurdity of my literal-mindedness but couldn't help myself, as the song fizzled to its end.

"Thank you," the director muttered unenthusiastically. "You may warm up for the dance number if you'd like. Next." No one that I could see had been listening, so no one clapped or said good job. The guy was trying to give a kid a break and I felt there was no reason for us to stay.

"Besides, I can't dance like these pros," I whispered to my father as we took our seats.

"Don't be silly. He's a little preoccupied after a full day of auditions, but he loved you! They're desperate for fresh young talent." My father was going to stick this one out to the bitter end.

"Then let's at least . . ."

"You are far and away the best performer I've seen here all day. You need some spit shine on your experience. Think what great training this will be for you. A next step." He was behaving as though the merest dimming trace of possibility were reins he held firmly in his hands. It had been decided. Anyone who cared to could have tasted the dusty wake of the winners who had pulled ahead.

Whatever my father thought I was growing up to be, this was the first time I remember thwarting his plans in front of him. I tripped over the alien movements, throwing the dancers beside me off by lifting my knees in their way. The stage could comfortably feature ten but not all thirty of us. I took up more room than most, and the choreographer threw his favorite male dancer in the front line a snide glance. Standing back, I watched him demonstrate the second combination. And five six seven eight. He landed and spun to face us with his hands out at shoulder height like putti wings. How could the others match his many counts to step and glide pivot lift, sight-reading once, then playing the tune in their perfectly syncopated bodies? Would no one else ask him to repeat? I stood behind a lithe, sure woman and watched the muscles of her buttocks change shape. Limber up, girl, I told myself, purple with chagrin. Count without moving your lips; may I sit down now?

"This is the kind of disappointment other girls have faced their whole lives," my father tried to reassure us both in the car before we left the parking lot. He had already transformed my negligible talent for song and dance into someone else's bad taste. "Only you're not like other girls," he said, adjusting his sunglasses in the rearview mirror while he started the ignition. "Don't ever forget that."

"You're not afraid to talk about it?"

"No.
It's such a long way off . . ."

"And was the death he died a hard one?"

"Dying's a cruelty to the unsuspecting. One needs strength
even for the deaths of those unknown."

"He was unknown to you?"

"Or: he's become so.
Death can estrange the parent from the child.
But it was dreadful during those first days.
All of my body was one wound."

—RILKE, "The Blind Woman"
(adapted from the C. F. MacIntyre translation)

7 / *M*y father, even though he was ill during my last years of high school, was preoccupied with my purity. Most of those last two years I was grounded for having come in late after the few dates I'd been allowed. He knew what happened after eleven o'clock and he was not going to allow his daughter to indulge. But it was not my classmates he needed to fear. He made up his mind that he was going to send me to a college he could trust, like Wheaton, where the pastor of our church and his wife had gone.

I thought of myself as a painter and had it in my head that I would go to the Ivy League school with the best art department. That was Cornell. Wouldn't he drive me there and see for himself if he was well by application time? I had worked hard for two years developing a portfolio I hoped was strong enough to qualify me for the school of my choice. The decision was mine as far as I knew. Because my father had been out of work, the guidance counselor thought I would get federal and state grants, which I did, and scholarships enough from Cornell to pay for room and board. The chairman of the art department called to congratulate me on my admission. He was looking forward to working with me in the painting program, he said. We drove up to Ithaca from our small Ohio town and I imagined my life in the spacious studios, with undraped models and prominent guest artists. I watched the postures and quick hands of the students in one morning class until the instructor asked a young man who had finished his work to show me around. My parents were taking a walking tour of the campus.

My designated guide was tall and slender, with soft-looking hair of a dark chocolate color. His eyebrows were thick but not too heavy and his brown eyes wore a bemused look, his head tilting a little when he asked my name. With an almost undetectable accent he said, "This way," and let me pass in front of him out the door. "I'll show you my favorite view in upstate New York. If it's still there. (Now I could place him.) I've been in Italy this past month visiting my father." Lucio, as he introduced himself, had brought back with him two flawless "stones" from the Buzzetti family marble quarry. I had not heard of that family but shook my head in amazement, knowingly. He was wearing suede pants and a loose-fitting white shirt. Glancing at me sideways as he talked, he wound our way through hallways and up stairs toward the top floor of the building until he found the right door. The room was empty. Its only windows were near the sloped ceiling, but they let in what seemed to me a glorious natural light. "To see my view you'll have to stand on a chair," he said. Not sure if this was a trick, I hesitated. "Go on," he urged, pulling a chair under the window for me. It was how he said it. I stood on tiptoe and could see all the way down into the fall-swept valley below to steeples and orchards and an open field of uncut dry grass. I felt his arm slip around my waist as he steadied himself on the chair behind me. "I want to see what you see," he said, and I could feel him breathing close to my ear.

My mind was made up. I was going to Cornell. "What do you like best about this place?" My parents were trying subtly both to introduce and to conceal their disapproval. Cornell had the highest suicide rate of all the Eastern schools, they'd heard.

"They told you that on your campus tour?"

"Well, one of the parents showed us the bridge where a girl from their town threw herself into the ravine during finals week," my mother admitted. They had also been shown the coed artists' dorms. No daughter of theirs was going to live like that. They liked Wheaton's unisex facilities. I could give it some thought. They would pray about it. It was settled.

My father and I could usually come to terms on major issues. Most often I would give in to his authority, but sometimes he gave me the sense that what I said provided him a new opportunity to see the world from a different, but eminently reasonable, point of view. I felt respected by my parents in ways that not many of my friends did. Not only did they listen, they were known to have changed their minds—on the matter of what church to attend, for instance; after sensing my enthusiasm, they visited the place I had been going on Sunday evenings since I could drive and liked it enough to stay. This mid-life change of churches had radically loosened their spiritual practice. So I kept approaching the matter of college from different angles. The angle of my future, what my teachers said, the level of education I could expect, how this was a once in a lifetime . . . On the angle of my father's missed opportunity, however, I had crossed the line.

"You can go to Cornell," he said, his eyes narrowing, "but you may not also consider yourself a daughter of mine." Nothing I had ever done had drawn from him the threat of my disinheritance. I could do it on my own; there was scholarship money. But without the blessing of my father I felt I had less of a chance of being blessed by God. To honor your parents—this is the first commandment with a promise—the verse ran through my head. The promise of long life. I would rather live short and fast, I felt, despising him for his ignorance. But I also fervently dreaded going out from under my father's approval.

On orientation day at Wheaton I gave up my grandmother's name for one given at birth to a girl I had admired that summer. She was a few years older than I was, a genuine flower child. I had taken the job as a counselor at a Salvation Army camp in the mountains of Pennsylvania after my failed amusement park audition. Smelling of patchouli in her gauzy skirts, she would bring me a single wildflower at breakfast. She had a tragic past. There were five other girls named Susan on the floor of my freshman dorm and I did not want to be associated in any way with anyone who would have chosen to be at this college. That was my excuse, though I must have harbored unexamined motives for wanting to be known as someone other than myself. There I was. I would have to make the best I could of things.

Wheaton is a very friendly campus. The upper classmen conducted a sort of unofficial welcome ceremony, sitting with foot-high numbers from 1 to 10 in the lobby chairs of the freshman dorm to rank the incoming girls. They recorded the ratings under our photos in the handbook given to all new arrivals, calling out our names as we lugged our boxes and trunks up the dormitory stairs. Susan Heche, they catcalled and whistled, fumbling over the pronunciation of my family name as I dropped my backpack off to the side of the door. I was miserable already. "That's a misprint," I lied over the noise. "My real name is Day. Day Heche." They wrote that in under my picture and conferred among themselves as to my score. I liked the pair of long A sounds together, though I hadn't thought before I said it about how the first name would fit together with my last. I don't remember having weighed the change at all, in fact, before I blurted out my metamorphosis, for in my mind that was what had happened. It was not long before almost everyone on campus called me by my borrowed name. You say it, and they believe it. This wouldn't be so bad.

I made cautious friends that first week of college with a young man I'll call Arthur. He had a sense of humor that made me laugh right through the seriousness of my incarceration. There were a few other unwilling consignees, artists and philosophy majors, students of music and literature, three young women in particular whom I grew to love. And sitting, enjoying the day's last sun, on the edge of the fountain I passed on my way to find the dining hall, was the boy I would later marry. We all introduced ourselves the very first day of freshman orientation, the odd lot of us disgruntled down to the food we were served. We passed our first year making overmuch of everything and then tentatively laughing at ourselves. Every one of us went home that summer thinking we would transfer, and one or two did. But inevitably almost all of us came back for more.

Our second year of school, after Arthur spent a long weekend with me at my parents' house in Ocean City, he broadcast to our circle of friends on campus that my father was a closet faggot. When I talked about my father in front of him, I could identify the ones he'd told by their exchange of covert glances. This was right before Arthur began confiding to a few of us his own sexual struggles. Maybe talking about my father helped him realize what happens if you play along. If it was so obvious, why didn't I see my father's cramped, ingrained agonies, which Arthur had detected?

The night the two of them stayed up late I had wondered what they had to talk about. In my head I went through all the other fathers I knew who could be considered effeminate, whose jobs weren't conventional, and my father kept coming up manly by comparison. Extraordinary. I loved the way his flouting of professional convention multiplied my choices. Of course I was still angry with him about school, but there was not a moment's hesitation on my part in rallying to his defense. End of story: it was Arthur's own proclivity that he read into everything.

And then, back on campus, it began snowing like crazy, a late November Lake Michigan squall. When I got back to the sophomore dorm, my roommate's boxes were all packed. The bathroom counter was cleared of her jars of hypoallergenic oils and shampoos. I ran down the hall to the resident director's suite and back to the room thinking, I will find out what's happening. This isn't happening. Surely she will be at dinner. She had wrapped her stereo and records in her old soft blanket and taken down the postcards and familiar sayings from her side of the room. *Water is the only truth of water. Water is water's complete virtue.* Solzhenitsyn Scotch-taped over Steinem. On my desk I found a piece of notebook paper with the words of Bob Dylan's "Forever Young" in her handwriting. Not here; so I threw my jacket back on and ran around campus to all the places we went, asking for her, looking. Not at special collections in the library, nowhere in the student center, bookstore, cafeteria; she must have been watching for me to leave, because when I returned from my search, her things were gone.

"You got too attached to her," Arthur said, still debating whether to come out of the closet. I'd cornered him in the campus post office, where he was already late to class. "She's exhausted by your too-too intensity, girl, like a lover she's not ready for." He looked at me for my reaction, putting his hands up around his neck as though he were being strangled.

"She thinks I'm a lesbian?" I had imagined the death of her father, who was diabetic, or a transfer from this school to another she hadn't wanted to tell me about until she was sure. "Just because you made up that story about my father being gay?"

"Not just, though I'm a good one to blame for most things," Arthur offered. He feigned a limp wrist and a lisp—"They do say that kind of thing is hereditary"—and went back to sorting through his mail for a letter that hadn't arrived.

"She couldn't even have waited till the end of the quarter?" My roommate and I had talked daily of transferring to schools on the East or West Coasts. She could have gone to Paris on the trail of a story, but not because of me. Because she thought I loved her, which I did. Who could blame me? She was the person I'd thought the most remarkable of any I'd known, in drive, in ideas, in her refusal of others' impositions. I cherished all the differences and likenesses between us. She was the one with red hair and powerful nails and a set of admirable unanswerable questions. I nursed my own set of innovations and rebellions, many of which she shared. Of course I was crazy about her.

Arthur, in a hurry but not one to neglect intrigue, proposed dinner, then suggested that I might be making too big a deal of things, as usual. "Back off, that's all. Besides, what would be so bad about being like me?" he chided. Arthur was seeing his sister's boyfriend on the side. We all strained under intensifying high jinks of sexual bewilderment. All I could figure out was that my friend (or was she?) was rattled by my asking her to pose for me so I could work on my figure drawing. Or she'd misread my fascination with David Hamilton's photographs of young women in fields wearing underclothes. I had shown her the collection in our favorite bookstore. His pictures seemed to me (I am ashamed to say I was taken with their soft-porn pandering) a dalliance with the female erotic that existed independent of male longing. I was initiating myself into the canonic texts of feminism and carried around a heightened but partial awareness of both my received limitations and my soaring capacities. Culling the admix of my intellectual stimulants, I was playing at androgyny. No one had yet written about the "hegemony of the gaze." My view of the image of two girls sheerly dressed, alone, did not take the camera into account. I took pleasure imagining myself there with them, uncensored, stretching before the mirror.

My roommate gave the photographs a quick glance and knew she had seen enough. She hurried over to the counter to buy an eraser and some sunflower seeds. We had been staying up all night arguing lately, discussing our futures. We were overthrowing traditional notions of doubt and faith and societally gendered roles and romantic dogma. She was a journalist, I was a painter. We were not turning in our papers on time or eating on schedule. When we did eat, it was vegetables and sugar-free dairy products, whole-grain breads.

For biology class I had been studying the principles of natural selection and adaptation (maybe that was what was going on, I wanted to tell her), how when two creatures of the same species with naturally similar needs and habits come together, in order to avoid competition, each goes to opposite extremes. They cancel out the middle ground. They emphasize difference. Our arguments were part of a greater terrestrial scheme. This was the biological process of coexistence by which a great enough diversity was gained, both geographically and behaviorally, to be able to live at peace on the same small island. However organic, I ached over the schism. She was not about to listen.

Maybe I was fooling myself. Sifting through those long days and nights for fragments of sexual adulation, I find instead the dream of a lifelong unfettered friendship between women, the promise of camaraderie and mutual trust. While I fed on notions of full disclosure, which I labeled "transparency," my ensuing invasiveness (understandably) made her squirm. She couldn't tell me directly, or was confused herself, when later I pressed her as to why she had left, why she couldn't see me for a while. She handled it like a breakup, ignoring me in the cafeteria, walking out of her way to avoid running into me, dropping our literature class. She tried to line up our circle of friends in the straight rows of her emotional precincts, and made herself generally unavailable for me to broach the subject of her fear of my sexual interest in her.

"It's like this," she said at our last lunch ever, a year or so later, when I had pressed her again to attempt some resolution. "When I get married, I'll be afraid that you will sleep with my husband." She was chewing her food when she said it, and then she wiped her mouth as if to finalize the thought. This was the reason for her abrupt bailout?

When I returned home to New Jersey for the Christmas break that year, I brought up the ordeal to my father as we were driving into Atlantic City to do some Christmas shopping. Careful to omit Arthur's rumor, which I was sure I must have mistakenly linked to the whole affair, I told him that I had always felt myself to be on the outskirts of campus life, looking on high-handedly. But after being shunned I had kept all the more to myself. From where I was sitting my father's eyes seemed to be almost laughing. He had a crookedly bemused smile on his face, part mocking, part identifying with me, or maybe with my accuser—I couldn't quite make sense of the look.

He had caught me once as a child playing doctor with the neighbor girl. Beside himself with anger to find me in the linen closet with her, he had shouted in front of my mother, after sending my friend home crying, "Do you know what they call people like you?" I was nine or ten. I shook my head. "They call them lesbians!" The word sounded like Vaseline, or caviar, revolting.

"Do you have those feelings toward her?" he now asked evenly, his smile still cryptic.

"I might," I said. "But I don't think so."

"You would know," he said. And I think I remember wondering how he could be so sure.

That holiday the gentleman teacher from the school for the deaf spent a good part of his vacation at our house with my brother Nathan, who was thirteen then and could hear perfectly well. At the time I had been conscious of my father's disdain for the fellow, who was twenty-seven, single, and "not a suitable friend for an adolescent," my father insisted. "He takes Nathan away from family time. They play cards for hours on end in Nathan's room." But what I overheard him calling the young teacher to my mother behind their bedroom door was a pervert. "Don't let our son spend unsupervised time with that pervert," my father said. "I have had a word of knowledge from God that the teacher is a homosexual." He spat out the word. "I'm going to have to have a talk with Nathan to let him know what's going on."

A word of knowledge was the sign of a special intimacy with God that manifested a finely tuned ear for truth. My father often posed as one so gifted as to receive portentous missives. Perhaps he was near to the heart of his heavenly father. Whatever special knowledge such identification of sexual bent took, he had it.

We'd finished hanging the white lights and mirrored roping on the tree. Since our first celebration of Christmas, when I was sixteen, my father had preferred a tasteful theme of ornaments to what he called the "traditional hodgepodge of family souvenirs." One year it was blues and purples. He spent hours wiring hand-tied bows onto branches already loaded with bunches of rubbery grapes and silk berries. The year my roommate left, it was crystal and mirrors and white-feathered birds that clamped onto the branches. In place of the star hung a mirrored dance-hall ball that cast its colorless glance about the room, absorbing from the spectrum as it turned. I was sitting in front of the fire gazing fondly from one relation to another, visually knitting each into a whole toward which the flames and the mirrors lent warmth. Mostly I was thinking about my own emotional states and upheavals, what it means to love, to marry, to be bereft, abandoned. But for a moment I was actually, purely, happy, which fatigued me. "Are you comfortable, sweetie?" my mother asked, seeking attention. I nodded, turning back to my book with a frown, half warmed by the fire, half resenting the way it drew everybody toward it.

Nathan and Dad had been arguing. There was some money missing from my father's dresser drawer and Nathan was the prime suspect. He had just stormed off to bed. Abigail, ever the cheerleader with long white-blond silk hair, backbending and splitting, spreadeagled in the middle of the air, came to land and poked at the embers. She pulled out one long strand of hair and drew a coal from under the flaming logs with the iron tongs.

"Hair stinks when it burns," she said, holding the scorched strand to her nose. She pulled out another strand of hair, deliberately, waiting for me to tell her to stop. The adults were going to talk; having gone away and come back, I was one of them. "My room's freezing," Abigail said. "I wish I could sleep right down here in front of the fire." That year fire's allure blazed at different heats for each of us. In some, the stale smell of ash would linger; in others, the embers only then began to flare.

8 / $\mathcal{I}$t was not until a few years later, after I was married and living in New York with a first child on one hip, that I could actually detect the free fall into which my family had, with a series of reflexive lurches, hurled their lives. There was no way I could have anticipated then just how far there was to plummet for us all. My father's business had deteriorated to pure and undeniable fantasy. My family had sold their house in Ventnor and moved to an apartment, then back into a beachfront house in Ocean City, where they were unable to pay the rent and so were unexpectedly locked out by their landlord and the sheriff one day. They clutched their suitcases on the wide porch, unable to think what to do, until one of the

children, who had run to a friend's house, showed up with an invitation for dinner and to spend the night, which turned into a week and then months of charity. The friends, generous beyond belief, doubled up in rooms and moved to attic bunks so that my family would have a home until the cycle of loss ended. Two families under one roof, shared meals and bathrooms, a houseful of teenagers. My mother would have to take a job. My father, under growing tension within and between families, would have to find alternative accommodations. His health had been deteriorating. What he had been calling cancer needed the constant care of his physicians in New York, so his move in with friends there muffled the disarray at home. His need for medical treatment appeared to be an adequate alibi for his leaving.

The week before he moved out I drove down from New York to talk with my father. I could only piece together from hurried calls my mother made from her office, where she worked as a stockbroker's assistant, what she and the other children were living through. Sitting at the kitchen table— we were having cereal together and I had to push the boxes out of the way so I could see him—he was talking to me about one of his deals and I knew from his antic gestures that whatever anemic doubts he had were trying to surface.

"We're flying down to Texas on Thursday for the first installment."

"Why don't they just wire you the money?"

"Wires can be traced. This involves governments that would prefer to remain anonymous."

"And you don't trust your partner to go alone?"

He practically choked on his corn flakes. "I suppose you know that I've been working nights at a club in Atlantic

City? I've been playing anywhere I know they need a piano player. For not much money, but what do you suggest I do? The church's small change hardly pays enough for gas. For bus fare up and back I can get a gig in New York."

I had been planning this encounter. I had steeled myself against the excuse of there being no real work in the world for him. He had been out of any kind of job for so long, living for at least three months by then with the family that had taken them in. He needed to find a place for his children to live. Could we stop pretending, please? If a child asks for bread, does her father give her a stone? It was time now. I called what I thought was his bluff.

He was too quick with cover even for himself. He was living the last months of his life and hadn't let on to anyone that he was dying. Tired maybe, run-down. He had a headache or a sore throat and thought he would rest.

"Your mother asked you to come, didn't she?"

"I came because I think you need to start thinking about another approach to earning a living. That's evident to anyone who bothers looking. I want to talk with you about your plans."

"Your mother has every right to despise me."

"Let's keep on the subject of you, Dad. This isn't about someone else's complaint. This is about the effect I see your choices having on your family." YOUR family, I say from the professional chair, not MINE.

He kept examining the moons of his fingernails. He didn't think it was my place to interfere like this. But then—and I don't know if what he said next was genuine or a lame show—his lips pulled back from his teeth and he sobbed once from his groin all the way up through his chest as though his throat would split, and he blurted out, "You could never imagine what a horrible husband I've been. You could never imagine."

My mother had pinned her ultimatums to the discussion between my father and me. If there were no changes made or begun after our talk—he listens to you—she wanted him out of there. The family they were staying with supported the idea of a temporary separation. The business of marriage, normally conducted in the privacy of one's own bedroom, under these conditions was overheard not only by the children but also by the host family at whose table we sat for meals and conferences. Decisions became a matter of community persuasion. How would the Heches live their lives? Don could find housing for himself, it was agreed. The rest of the family was welcome for as long as they needed a home. It was Christmas. If he didn't have a job within a month, he was on his own.

With my mother's work and the children's pooled contribution from babysitting money and ice-cream dipping on the boardwalk, pizza delivery and help at the fruit and vegetable market after school, they could soon afford a small apartment. It felt good to be able to pay the rent and utilities and still have money for food. This was temporary. We had never lived within our means the way they did then. I could see, when I visited, the pride they felt in their self-reliance, and their increasing resentment of a husband and father who had only schemes to contribute.

"How is he?" I asked my mother. "Do you two talk at all these days?"

"You could say we talk." The color rose around her temples. "Last month I paid off the remainder of his $900 phone bill so that we could get our service restored. I tell you, if I don't cut the ties soon, his debt is going to bury me."

I could picture her slow suffocation. "Would a legal separation protect you at all, you know, from creditors?" I said.

"Why delay the inevitable?" she asked, throwing a hot pad into the tiny kitchen sink for emphasis. "It's not that I don't care for him, who wouldn't, it's . . . I've talked to a lawyer at work about filing for divorce." She started for the back door and I followed her out onto the landing, where she had carried a chair, and sat down.

"Have you talked about this with Dad?"

"I've told him I want to see other men. Twenty-five years I've been faithful to him, he ought to know. Could he say the same? I'm starting to wonder. Thick and thin, all that, sickness and health."

"What did he say?"

"He read me the riot act—hyperventilating on his hospital bed. Unfaithful, he called me. To what?"

I'm thinking, She needs to put some time between my father and another man, for her own sake, for the impressionable children she still has at home. She's telling me to ask my permission, I know. This year I have been the parent in my own mind, the one thread of connection to her former life, holding forth, like so much smoke blown in my parents' faces, the virtues they had trained me to honor. She expects me to scold her.

"What men? Jim, Ed? Some other strain of South Jersey fever?" I say, stepping down and up on the wooden stairs. She runs her fingernail under some loose paint on the railing. I am from Ohio, raised on a defunct system of laws and prohibitions that my parents had begun to shed on their conversion to the coast.

"This needs painting, too." She says it with disgust, not accustomed to surroundings so affordable. I'm stationary on the step now, waiting. "I haven't talked about him because I knew you wouldn't approve. But I'd like you and Judson to have dinner with us tomorrow night."

Us. They were already a coalition. They had planned an evening together on one of the few nights I could be at home and had presumed my interest in being there with them. What must she have told him, whoever he was, about my father? I was supposed to go out on a date with my mother and her boyfriend while her husband was convalescing?

"I've never been much for double dates, thanks"—my response was snide but well deserved, I calculated. She could see whomever she liked. I had come to see my brother and sister perform in the high-school play, anyway, and Dad was supposed to come down from New York if he was feeling well enough. My mother's anger was becoming high-pitched. How unfair I was being. Why did I insist on withdrawing when she needed me the most?

"I'm going to have friends, aren't I? I would have thought you'd be interested in meeting them, just as I have always valued the people you've had in your life."

"Boyfriends, I think you mean," I said, trying not to let her get away with euphemisms for her recent infidelities. "You've always liked my boyfriends."

The night of the play, the night of the proposed dinner, I steered clear of her apartment, making plans instead to spend the early evening with my grandmother in the rooms she had rented to be near my mother for a while. She had offered to watch the baby while I went to the play with my father, but when I got to her place my mother answered the door with her date peering over her shoulder. They had just finished jogging and had stopped by. What a surprise! So my grandmother was in on the conspiracy. The couple shone with sweat, their short shorts matching. My mother was wearing a new pair of jogging shoes I knew she couldn't afford.

"So, Susan; almost exactly how I'd envisioned you," the date said. His hand was hairy and moist. "I'm the culprit, Alan." My mother had begun a practice I've always resented in regard to the men she's dated since that time. They seem to know the gist of every recent conversation I've had with her, but never the substance of my principles. She repeats to them what she remembers and omits my main point.

"Hello, Alan," I said, looking at him and trying not to go immediately into defensive postures with my arms or jaw.

"I understand you are a young woman with high standards," Alan says. He wants to delve right in, doesn't want anyone to mistake him for a shy person. My husband picks up a book, walks into a back room, and closes the door. My mother has ushered my grandmother into the kitchen and left me alone with her date in the living room. Whatever he wanted he wasn't going to get from me, on his terms, against my expressed wishes.

"High standards." I consider the notion. "My mother gave her discards to me," I say.

"We all have our sources." He thinks this is smart talk.

I can tell he feels smart about every word he utters. My grandmother hurries back into the room with orange juice in tall glasses, just in time to prevent me from telling Alan what I think of my mother and what a mess she is making of her life. My grandmother is talking about happiness, about each of us deserving happiness, chattering away.

"Don't you think your mother deserves her happiness, too?" she asks the general listening audience, including Alan. She smiles at Alan as if he is the answer she has been looking for to fulfill her own future security and my mother's well-being. I adore my grandmother but suddenly despise the way she softens her tone of voice when she is talking in the presence of a man. "Do you think your mother deserves less than what's best for her, Susan?" she presses. She has turned to me with her tray of refreshment and I take a glass gingerly. This is a movie I did not rehearse for, the characters changing mid-script. My mother forces a laugh, off camera. Alan searches his mental cavern for a witticism and opens his mouth, but then raises his glass in slow motion and takes a gulp of juice. My mother lays her hand on Alan's arm as if to draw him toward the door. He ignores her.

"Susan, you are in many of our conversations, many conversations between your mother and myself. Nancy, I think I'll stay if you approve, but you may go home and shower if you prefer." Alan is telling my mother what to do and she likes this. He has so much to tell me, too, for the record. To set some things straight, to justify his presence. My baby has been fussing in the back bedroom with Judson. It's time to eat and get ready to go to the play. When I look at my watch my mother brushes the dark hair on Alan's arm coaxingly; another time, her eyes plead, and

Alan takes a deep breath. "Well," he says, and then relents.

"You two have a great evening," I say. "You deserve it!"

Outside the high-school auditorium I bought tickets for the performance and waited for my father to arrive. Judson was home with the baby. My grandmother came with me but didn't care to sit with my father, she decided after a few moments of standing by the drinking fountain. She would find a seat if I would wait for her after the show.

He came in twenty minutes into the first act, playing blithe spirit, looking quite well despite several recent bouts with surgery. I think we must have hugged each other, and then I listened to the gory details, the costs, the story of the train ride through Morningside Park or around it, and his near brush with death as he exited the subway at 116th below the park. I did not like to think of him dying. "I'm glad you made it," I said. This would not be so difficult, after all. We had a lot to catch up on of our own that could circumvent the family issue.

"If you get a chance"—at intermission he became a theater critic advising me with broad gesticulations as to Broadway fare—"see *Sophisticated Ladies*. The *Cotton Patch Gospel* is terrific. We only stayed for the first half— I was with clients—but you'll love it. It's a fairly quiet show. Harry Chapin's music set to drama, that sort of thing." He carried a small black Sportsac with him, over one shoulder. He was on his way as soon as the curtain fell. He would see Abigail and Nathan after the show, of course, then head back to the city for some meetings. What all could he fit into that bag?

The cast members came out into the school corridors

to greet their audience after the show. Their makeup had congealed around the edges of their faces with the heat of the lights and the overreaching display of their dance routines. Abigail and Nathan scanned the crowd for Dad, who had been gone so long—was it good riddance they felt or a yearning for him? They took turns defending and despising him. That night Nathan's was a quick greeting; he had to run, things to get off stage, but thanks for coming. But Abigail would not let our father go. I watched her hug him as though nothing or everything were wrong, forever, a long long hug between the two of them. A path of tears channeled through the layers of pancake and dripped in skin-colored globules onto his sweater. My grandmother watched too, silently, trying unsuccessfully to harden the look on her face, and went to stand by the door.

The next day enormous flower arrangements, one for each of his children who had been in the play, arrived at the high school before lunch. Abigail walked home holding the round glass vase out from her body so the flowers wouldn't crush. Nathan gave his away.

Where my father had been living is something I learned only recently from Abigail. It was during that period, she told me, that she would meet Dad in a house where he stayed in Atlantic City when he was not in the hospital or with friends in New York. She would take the bus after closing up at the fruit and vegetable market and buy him and his friends dinner on money she had stolen from the cash register drawer. His friends were brothers, my father told her. Two brothers he had met through business in New York.

"We would have elegant, flaming desserts," Abi

said, "and then walk them off. They were as worried about the calories as I was. We would all hold hands. It had a family feel to it, I guess, stretching across the whole width of the boardwalk, railing to railing. Dad needed money, so I took it."

The house my father stayed in was one that had been on the market for a while without selling, priced as it was out of most buyers' reach. He worked when he could for the realtors who had listed the house and so had keys available. Because the house was furnished, he could make believe it was his own to visitors. My sister kept up her end of his cover, their unspoken compact, and hung some of her clothes in the closet of the bedroom that would have been hers. It was a beautiful house, like the one he would buy when his deal closed.

"Dad and I got along so well in those days," Abi told me, her ironic tone full of defeat. "He used to promise me he would give me a bigger piece of the pie when his deals came through because of all I'd done for him. 'You're the only one of my children who's cared for me while I've been in this slump,' he'd tell me." She whimpers a little, pretending to be a wounded puppy. "Like a dummy I believed him." She can't think of a single dear memory of him, not one time he loved her like the father she imagines having loved in return.

Anne had met one of the brothers, too. There was a party at his house one night when she had ridden the bus up from Ocean City. My father had told us that he worked on the staff at a church which ministered to the gay community." They could come in drag. He made a space (my father assisting with the punch and cake) for people who needed to be loved.

Anne told me of one man who believed himself a prophet, a handsome thirty-five-year-old. He came up to her—she thought to introduce himself—and laid his hands on her head, inviting her to pray. "I have had a vision of your father," he told her, his tone ecclesiastical. "God has revealed to me that your father will be healed, completely." She could not move her head in any direction. "He gave me an image of your father's illness falling off his body like an iron cast. A perfectly whole man lives inside. Say thank you to God, Anne." The only way out of the room was to say it. She was fourteen. She ducked out onto Seventh Avenue to catch her breath.

We saw him those days one at a time, Abigail on an occasional weekend when he went back to Atlantic City to flip burgers for some spare change. "A fag-hag ran the place," she remembers. "I would go and sit at the counter in this dark, narrow hole-in-the-wall, having a Coke, or fries or something. And he would carry greasy burgers between the grill and the booths of nuzzling male regulars."

Nathan, when he could not avoid his father, took the brunt of a sick man's self-loathing. If it wasn't for Nathan's starting that fire in the stairwell at the oceanfront condominiums, my father insisted, our family could have lived there indefinitely. Whatever possessed him—he had always been bad news. And now the other residents wanted nothing to do with them. If it wasn't for Nathan's lateness, his laziness, his eating habits, his poor taste, wild, execrable—irrationally my father connected my brother's existence to his own dereliction—what couldn't he have achieved?

Anne rode the bus from Ocean City to New York and back for auditions, a commercial spot paying her way, or a child's part in a dinner-theater play. She would stay with

Dad in the large, church-attached apartment, where he fixed her breakfast, and they would sleep in the same double bed in a room off the high-ceilinged living room, where at night Mr. Stuart and our father entertained guests.

During the day, after she had made her rounds, they would meet for a soda at an appointed corner and she would walk him home (between them they could not afford a taxi), holding him up when he grew weak, sitting down on the sidewalk with him if he collapsed. He was alert in unreplenishable bursts which momentarily capped the sea of fatigue that seemed to have engulfed him. On each visit he had visibly deteriorated. They would make it to the church and he would take off his clothes, draping them over a chair. After helping him into the bed they shared, she would work on lines for the next day's auditions and then fall asleep herself, awkward beside his nakedness.

After my father had moved away from the family, I had wanted to lend what support I could to my mother as she raised my brother and sisters by herself. My father seemed to crave his independence and to guard himself from even my most casual inquiries. Because he was in and out of the hospital in Manhattan and I lived in Yonkers, I was close enough, and the hospital was neutral enough territory, for me to see him there a few times, which felt to me like approving his familial negligence. Was it up to me to take sides? Had he included me in his abandonment? He didn't have the strength or inclination to consider anyone else. The time before the last time I visited him at Bellevue, he had grown so frail that the sight of him eclipsed my notion of him as provider. That would be my role now,

a part for which he must have found me lacking, whatever
I offered.

Surely it is best to be incautious with charity. Better
that than begrudging, but over the years so many well-
intentioned people fed my father's weakness with their gifts.
Bankers loaned him money for a Cadillac. Real-estate
agents let the family stay temporarily in vacant furnished
houses on the oceanfront. The deacons of the church co-
signed for mortgages and later contributed toward heating
bills and food. Near the end, his charm exhausted and the
well of generosity he'd drawn from overtapped, my father,
penniless, simply took what he could get. Where there was
instant credit at department stores he'd purchase gifts for
himself and others up to his limit. This is what my sisters
wore to their proms—costly gowns "bought" from unsuspecting New York store clerks he'd given a false address.

One morning in February my phone rang. An older
woman's voice I'd never heard launched right into what
she'd called to say.

"I don't know who you are," she trilled, "but whoever
is calling you long distance from the city and charging it
to my private line had better quit."

"Did you get my number from your phone bill?" I
asked.

"Yours, and about a dozen or so others I have never
in my whole life dialed." Mine was evidently the closest to
Manhattan, so she'd called me first. I knew immediately
this was my father's doing.

"Who would be using your number, do you think?"

"That's why I'm calling you, young lady! To find out!

There are area codes from all across the country. These are very long calls, not simply hello and goodbye. I have no idea what to do with this bill: Texas, California, Long Island; here's one to Ocean City, New Jersey."

I should have offered to pay for the calls made to my apartment, but she was not a pleasant woman. Her tone of voice accused me of her trouble. I didn't think to offer until after I'd hung up, and she had been reluctant to let me know her name or where she could be reached. I should have asked for the list of other numbers. That would have been a record I could have used, though at the time I wasn't sure I wanted it.

Shortly after that call, I saw my father on Madison Avenue, where I was walking with my baby. We had been to an exhibition at the Metropolitan and were headed, my son bundled in his snowsuit in the portable stroller, to a restaurant for lunch. My father was wearing the summer-weight navy suit I had seen him in the last time he had been out of his hospital gown. He looked tanned or, rather, jaundiced, but less skeletal than before.

"Of all things! To run into you on the street today! Let me buy you lunch," he offered jovially.

"How great to see you looking so well," I said. This would be his last day out of bed. He had asked his doctors to let him leave the hospital to conduct some urgent business and they'd acquiesced. But by the time we made it to the restaurant where he wanted to take us he could barely stand. We had progressively slowed our pace as we'd walked. The wind whipped the avenue's debris around our faces. I could hear him gulping for deeper breaths between sentences, but the food revived him a little. He'd ordered

split-pea soup, which he fed the baby from his own spoon.
I think I had a chicken-salad sandwich.

When the bill came, my father immediately picked it
up and looked it over carefully. As we stood to go he reached
first into one back trouser pocket and then felt in the other.
Goodness, had he misplaced his billfold? Before he could
pretend to have been robbed, his face already wearing an
exaggerated puzzlement as he slipped his hand into his
inside jacket pocket, I grabbed the check, slow on the up-
take, and paid what we owed.

*And secretly, in my heart, I would gnaw and nibble and probe
and suck away at myself until the bitter taste turned at last
into a kind of shameful, devilish sweetness and, finally, down-
right definite pleasure. Yes, pleasure, pleasure!*
— D O S T O Y E V S K Y , *Notes from the Underground*
(translated by Jessie Coulson)

9 /　　　　　　　*D*id your father die young?"
my older son, Elliot, asks me as I'm tucking him into bed.
He is a natural piano player with the kind of musical touch
my father was born with.

"Yes, he did. He was forty-five years old."

I show him the photograph I have in my notebook of
my father lying on the sofa at the beach house with his shirt
off and a newborn baby propped in the crook of his arm.

"That's you when you were one month old." He ex-
amines the photograph, taking care not to touch the surface.
He has no memory of his grandfather: I haven't talked
about him much with my children.

My father looks so young. His arm curves protectively

around the sleeping child, whose open hand rests on my father's chest. He was ill already at the time, though his color is good. If you knew him you can see his vigor has begun to fade, yet he doesn't look remotely frail. We thought it was ordinary stress. "I'm exhausted," he would say over and over, not complaining but annoyed. The telephone is propped beside him just in case, and the sun seeps through the drawn vertical blinds that shade them from the heat of the day.

"What made him die?" Elliot has been curious about adult conversation for a while now. He often lingers at the dinner table to listen when the other children run off to play. I glance from my husband, who has just looked in to say good night, back to my ten-year-old son.

"He died of cancer," I tell him. In my mother costume I do not elaborate: skin cancer and pneumonia, the common cold, hemorrhage of the brain, thrush, sex, shame. The most agonizing of deaths, one calamity on the back of another. After he fell from bed he died of the fall, unable to recover.

"Oh, that's what I thought." He turns his face into the pillow.

My visitor's pass said 16N49B. He was not in his room, so I was encouraged that he had been able to walk someplace, needed to get out, and could. Even pneumonia he had found the strength to rise above. I asked a nurse wheeling a cart of medicines and turquoise plastic pitchers down the hall where the patient lounge might be. "Either end," she barked. I walked behind her, peering into rooms as I passed. There was a man alone in a room, facing out the window which overlooked the East River and Roosevelt Island, the boats, the traffic heading downtown.

"Could this be his room?" I called to the nurse, seeing that the numbers on the door and on my pass didn't match.

"Well, is that him?" she said over her shoulder. "Take a good look."

If it was not my father I didn't want to intrude on another of the patients, to be caught staring, as if at their indigence. If hollow eyes needed to be met, I wanted to save my initial sympathies for him. I looked from the man to the nurse until he turned aggravatedly toward the hall, straining to see that far into the distance. My father.

He had never been robust, but he had dropped thirty-five pounds since the last time I had seen him just weeks before. His head looked as if it had grown for a moment before I recognized the effect of his shrunken body, wrinkled with the loss, braced behind a tray in a vinyl-covered chair. He released a heavy breath and swallowed at the same time, which sounded like a sob as he choked out greetings, laboring to be alert and hospitable and to breathe all at once.

"I can't believe it. What a surprise." I think he cried those two sentences. I sat on the stool his feet were propped on and reached for his legs as he dropped them onto the floor to clear room for me. He listened to me fumble through a much longer sentence or two myself about having a pass to the wrong room and was the rest of the hospital service to his liking and . . .

"Are you glad, is it okay for me to be here, Dad?"

"Of course, I'm so very, very glad to see you." His voice was not strong enough possibly to convince. His face wrestled to keep back the tears which fell despite his efforts.

"Are you lonely here?" What kind of inane question was that, coming from my mouth one minute into my visit out of the blue? As though I were talking to a child who didn't hear well, I repeated myself. "Are you feeling lonely?"

"No, no. I'm just fine." He looked lonely, I guess, and tired. "I need the rest, that's all, the time and the rest. I am so tired. So exhausted these days. This is the longest I've been off the oxygen for a week." He turned to the view. "Gorgeous view," he said. We spoke of the river for a while, and the bridge and the island. I tried to coax his feet back onto the stool beside me. No, he would rest them on the wastebasket, sit, sit. I couldn't think of anything else to do to try to make him more comfortable. What was it, fluff the pillows, make crisp corners of the sheets while he's out of the bed?

"It's three o'clock," I offered.

"What a fiasco this has been"—he was reviving— "from being carried in on a stretcher to trying today from nine in the morning until just before you got here to get a glass of water." At least he could still blame others for his condition. I prompted his gripe about the food, the nurses, to reassure him that I wasn't there to discuss family matters, his business, his health.

"Let's just sit here for a while, Daddy. I'll get you some water and then we can just sit."

"No, please sit down, I need to talk." How uncharacteristic of him. I saw as he licked his lips to wet them that his tongue was a thick yellowish slab.

"Do you have all you need in the way of toothbrush, shaving cream, things like that?" I began the list of toiletries he would need in my head and opened his bedside-table drawer. There was another hairpiece and a tape of the Off Broadway show he had been playing for before being hospitalized. I turned over a box of imported raspberry candies and found some loose coins underneath. "I'll bring you some juices and tea bags." Vitamins, toothpaste, oranges, Cup-A-Soup: he was describing his liquid diet restrictions while I took notes.

He told me about his night on a stretcher in the emergency room alongside all the pushers, gunshot victims, and near-dead drunks. " 'Listen, bud,' I shouted at one particularly noisy bastard, 'I am as sick as you are, so shut up, turn over, and go to sleep,' at which the fellow complied." In a roomful of those suspended over life's precipice, waiting to be lured back from the edge, or simply longing to heave themselves into a painless oblivion, my father was, for that one night, where he belonged.

Then the operation story: a grueling day of tests, tubes through the nose and down into the lungs; in the haze of anesthesia he could hear the doctors saying over him, "There, just go a little deeper now. Scrape from the lower lobe, in that lower corner there." All around, a circle of students watched the biopsy.

"My throat was so sore. I had said to the doctor on the way into surgery that this was such an act of faith, putting your life in the hands of someone you have only just met. He told me I would be glad I had. I vomited all over my bed when I came back up to my room and they didn't even change the sheets until today. Three days later." He held up his fingers. His complaint was agitating him. He had to stop to catch his breath before going on.

"But the doctors here, now that's another story, only the best. You know, this is a research hospital, much like the place I had my medical training. The doctors have treated me like one of them, really. My two main specialists are the teaching residents, so they're no slouches. They come around here with their students to poke at my liver or we exchange jokes." He reached for a single piece of paper in his drawer, then squinted at the words one of the doctors has evidently handwritten for him. He read *Pneumocystis carinii*, and smiled at his precision. "They call it PCP. It's like Legionnaire's disease, they told me. How you catch it is a mystery. Though they assure me I'm noninfectious."

Still the hype, the keeping up of appearances—only the best—which I thought would have been wrung out of him with this latest deterioration. His minister friend had told me that, on the way into the hospital, Dad had turned to him and confided that he felt exhilarated tonight, he felt he'd rounded the bend. He'd received a call from London saying that the payment for his latest service was transferring banks. Relief, when the house where he had been staying was now occupied by its owners, and his money consisted of the change under the candy box in his hospital room. No watch, no car, and his oldest child sitting there wondering if it would ever be the right time to break the news to him of his family's jeopardy.

Mr. Stuart had spared no details to impress on my mother the need for my father to be committed into the hands of doctors who could give him the care he needed. "He couldn't breathe, walk, open his eyes. It took us half an hour to walk the two blocks from one doctor to another on Park Avenue the other day. He was that weak." Mr. Tweed was pleading with her, as if she had some decision to make.

Here lay the man I knew as Don Heche. There is something deceptive about the body. He wanted to shower. If I would run out for some rations, he could clean up while I was gone. I came back from the deli to a cat-bathed father, straightened hair, clean beard, soap by the sink having to double for shampoo. The hospital had provided that when he had asked. I arranged all the food on his cabinet shelf: pudding, fruits, soups to make instantly in boiling water.

"I'll be able to let hot water run in the sink to fix that up. They don't bring boiling water around, or even check the water in the oxygen setup very often."

Reading material was out of the question. He had been glancing at an issue of last year's *Life* magazine before I had walked in and even the pictures were too much for his eyes. They had weakened, we both hoped not permanently. He was failing with the exertion he felt was called for with me in the room, so I helped him to his bed and sat next to him while he filled up on oxygen again. He motioned for me to look away; it embarrassed him to have the mask over his face in front of me. I turned for his benefit, to look out the window or into the hallway.

My father had met a man the other night, he said, who used him as a sounding board. "A free psychiatrist, you know." The way he described the fellow, with care for the details and contempt for his troubles, I thought he might be talking about himself. "He needs professional care," my father was saying. "I am in no way qualified to unscrew all the tangled mess inside him, but he wasn't particular. His hang-ups go as far back as his father, his unwelcome child-hood. But I listened. I guess it helps to be able just to let it all out for some people. I should have given him a mirror. That would have cut right to the quick, wouldn't it?"

How to love this man, my father, I'm wondering, who

taught me to scorn failure. I make a cup of tea with hot tap water. I trade the broken tray resting on his bed for the one across the room. "Here is my phone number on your Klee-nex box if you want to talk with me, even if you don't need anything. Or if you do." I've written large numbers and show him to make sure he can read them. "Or if you don't want to call . . ." I mutter to myself. He is barely breathing now. I go hunting for a nurse, and when we come back he has propped himself up on one elbow.

"Don't bother to come back here again, sweetie. I know you're busy with Judson and the baby," he gasps. The nurse fidgets with the oxygen machine, untangling the tube with audible impatience. Does he want to see me? Or does he think I was put out by coming? "We can get together when this is all history." He lets his head fall back against his pillow and speaks up toward the ceiling. "It's hard for you to get downtown. I'll be fine. Just fine."

March 5, 1983, fifteen days before he would have turned forty-six, my father's older sister calls me from the hospital. She had driven from Indiana too late to see him, and when I heard her voice I knew. "Is he dead?" I ask her. "What day is it?" Shouldn't my mother have been the one to know first, to have been called? "Are you giving them his body?" They were having it shipped intact to In-diana. The burial would be in a few days. They had yet to make arrangements. "Does my mother know?" My father's sister thought so, though she didn't quite understand what terms she and my father were on that my mother was not offering to pay for the funeral.

The burial wasn't hard: one body for one grave, next to his father. The March dirt was still frozen. In Chicago a

blizzard grounded all the planes, so I was spared the low-
ering of the box, denied the finality that might have freed
me from the dream of his candor.

He has been dead ten years and finally I have found
some of my father's other life, parts of him remembered by
those who didn't know us, or who did and thought it best
to cover for him—the ones who left the candy in his bedside
drawer, the numbers he called and charged to a stranger's
telephone. On the way to finding him I called his business
associates whose names I could remember—dead men—
whose widows answered the phone and spoke with bitter-
ness at their betrayal. How had my mother found out, they
wondered; how was she taking it?

I spoke with wives of my father's friends who don't yet
know about their own husbands. Pretty women with sad
expressions beneath their good humor, and years of un-
asked questions and debts. These men all live beyond their
means. A friend of mine saw one of the husbands in a gay
bar telling stories, surrounded by his peers. She stood too
far away to hear his words, watching his exaggerated gesticulations. He looked thinner than he had before. When
their eyes met, he pretended not to know her (she was there
with her brother), to be someone else (it had to be him),
though just a week ago they had sat across the table from
each other at a dinner party. He finished his story with
studied casualness, telling his circle not to look now; they
all laughed too loudly. Taking the arm of the man nearest
him, the man's body his only defense now, he headed toward the rear of the bar. She did not pursue him. To say
hello, recognizing him, would have been to intrude.

I'm beginning to think the closet men must be more susceptible. They go down so easily, their immune systems already overtaxed by the exertion of living two lives in a single body.

I talked with a survivor of the eighties gay scene in New York who knew my father then, and with the lesbian couple who owned the paintings. People who would talk with me were not so difficult to find once I was willing to listen.

Each one had been part of the unspoken resolution to keep quiet when he was alive. But that was then, ten years ago, and another climate, less tolerant, or without the current pressure toward acceptance. Now, with him out of hearing range or recourse, their thoughts could be as full of speculation as mine. Someone might provide a fact, a place, a name, a picture of him visible in the meager description over the phone, or between us in a noisy café. What was he wearing; what did they remember him saying? Did he talk about himself? Had he known what he was doing?

There were others whose relationships with my father I left alone, or only mildly pursued. I tried to respect unreturned phone calls after leaving several messages. Certain closets I only toyed with forcing open. The summer we had moved to Indiana to care for my father's parents he had stayed out late some nights with no explanation. My mother hadn't pressed him for an answer. Though years later, after he was already dead, my grandmother told her she had seen my father on occasion, late at night, with the man who played the organ at the Methodist church. The old organist had lived in town for many years with the man who ran the sound and lighting at the church. The community "understood" their relationship by ignoring it. The two of them and my father were old acquaintances, I discovered.

As an adolescent, learning to play the organ, my father had practiced at the Methodist church. There, in the house of God, a young man experiencing the overwhelming draw of music could have had—whether by coercion or magnetism, by example or as an initiate—his own sexual and spiritual awakening. The tangle of faith and sex and music in my father's life unraveled back and back until his early experiences appeared as single threads in the tight knot of his adult years. Often when my father played a hymn, tears would stream down his face. Is it joy? I asked him once. Is it sadness?

All that happens in the flesh, my father had taught me, has a correlative in eternity—the way we behave toward one another, the kind of language we use. The visible world is an earthly symptom of the world to come. Blessed are the pure in heart, for they shall see God. What we loose here will be loosed in heaven, what we bind will be bound. Had he changed his mind as his body disintegrated? Was it the other way around? Did he think that he would "pass away" (in the soft padding of euphemism), a soulless, corporal sediment?

In part because of my father's moral guardianship, his strictures on my sensuality, I don't get it, quite, when his queer friends talk to me about sex for its own sake, the kind of free-for-all nameless overexposed take-it-and-run sex of the late seventies and early eighties in New York. Sex has to *mean* something.

I found one man in particular who knew my father and

also knew our family. He had been a guest at the beach house before we lost it. I had considered him a good friend of mine—one of my favorite people. But he was a person for whom my father's death was a dividing line that put him on the other side. Renewing contact ten years later, we both expressed surprise that we had lost touch and relief to be together again. We rushed at the past to reconstruct, filling in the intervening years in a jumbled gush: my children (I never pictured you a mother of four), his lovers, our studies and travels, best books, dead ends. One of the last times I had seen him had been at my wedding, so we start there.

"I've dined out on the story of your wedding, darling. In some ways I've been obsessed with the Heche family. I have that Christmas card with the picture of all of you hanging on my wall. I remember it was a rainy day and Don was scrambling into a Cadillac so afraid that someone would see your dress before the big moment. Like he's going to art-direct the whole event—the fecundity of the young couple, your mother in a cream Versace bondage dress, this 1930s beaded gold-and-silver sheath of a gown with a poof for a veil that you finally appeared in on your father's arm. Don's fabulous wife and daughters and adorable son and his fabulous house and trimmed beard like an extension of his own fabulous . . . (I'm so elated to talk with you I'm working myself into a fit!) There were you and Judson, a couple of freaks . . ."

"Freaks?"

"For me that's a term of praise. Either you're vanilla-ville, the beige of nothingness, or you're . . . I was enriched by knowing you. You were all part of this nut house with a compelling, vibrant energy, but fucked up somewhere.

Then I lose track. And then I hear about the wallop. Something did go so amazingly bad, Susan."

"We're finally getting around to talking about it. I know what happened from my perspective, but not much about what my father's life must have been like—the part we didn't see. I thought you might be able to help me understand him a little."

"So you're outing the dead! Sure, let's talk, with the understanding that one homosexual can't speak for another, any better than one Caucasian can stand in for the race. But I'll tell you what my experience has been if that's relevant."

I feel nothing but anticipation. It feels so good not to be avoiding the unknown. How hard can this be?

"Your father never swiped at my crotch, or anything, when I was in your house. His hand may have lingered a little long on my shoulder at times, or he could have been too kindly offering to loan me his sweater or jacket. I always traveled light, poor, you know. That night we all drove down to Atlantic City and watched the Miss America pageant on the boardwalk, he wanted to be in the closet with me helping me on with his clothes. Remember we had those great seats your father had rustled up, I suspected from the Mafia or something? Now that was a trip—Miss Ohio, Miss California! But I was shaky about my sexuality at the time and he didn't press me."

"Just a hunch, then?" Not that I doubt him, but I'm trying to move from innuendo into something hard, details. How far had my father taken it?

"There was this kind of aura—a buzz—that made me very nervous—a tension. I was excited by it. We call it gay radar. You can smell another queen, especially in unlikely settings. Like dogs. Excuse the lingo—it's our speak—maybe I'm showing off for you."

The friend comes from the same kind of closet my father did—a fundamentalist Christian background and its prohibitions. A severely conflicted faith. Self-destructive, he fought himself before coming out. But he's younger than my father, never married, and is HIV-negative at the time of our talk. He keeps telling me how lucky he feels to be well. How no matter what kind of trip he's been on, he's had the presence of mind to keep sex safe.

"I knew your father in the late seventies and 1980, '81, when the pre-AIDS gay ethos was going full tilt. He seemed only a little less green than I did. You walked around the Village and saw these guys with their arms around each other, jeans half unbuttoned and their pubic hair hanging out. Everybody was fucking everybody. Sex was too available and I was too shut off from how to enter the sexual marketplace. I didn't want to get fist-fucked, but I did want to have a boyfriend."

Drawn into what he calls the "drama of external genitalia," he learned to flaunt it in the full comfort of camp. Are you cute? Are you funny? How famous can you get? Have I read Susan Sontag on the subject? The ongoing improvisational comedy feels like a liturgy, but you're a million miles away. The hollower the better. It all happens so slowly, he says, over a long period of time.

"We don't just morph into a new being in a second. First I had these fantasies of giving someone a blow job—coercion, not of my own volition. It's not my fault. When I met my first real lover and got comfortable with rimming and fucking and being fucked and having sex three times a day, I went from suicidal to full all-out like I never knew it existed before sex.

"I hadn't known it could be so totally wonderful. You know, the defining thing about being gay is that you like to have sex a lot. The need for sex creates itself out of sex you have or haven't had. You're always upping the ante. It's wild. It's zippy: you think, Just go for it. Coming from a moral structure heightens it. You know you're being bad.

"Then in 1988 I met Gordon, my current love. He's an oil scion from Texas. He introduced me to the A list of gay New York, and for two years we were on a tear. Dinner, pot, dancing, drinking, more pot, cocaine, 2:30 in Houston, Berlin. At the bathhouses we would wander from room to room, shopping. Some sad guys would be lying on their bellies with their butts up in the air. (We say, 'The guy who gets fucked is the guy who dies.' He sorta takes the female role, I figure.) I guess you could say Gordon was the pimp, I was the talent. He made the arrangements (again it's not my fault), while I tripped off to refill our drinks. It's like playing hooky or something. Your life hangs somewhere between day and night."

"You're invisible?"

"Remember Erica Jong's 'zipless fuck'? Sex unencumbered by commitment or thought? It's very powerful. If you allow it to get hold of you at all, you just want more of it. Some people's only capacity for transcendence is through sex, you know, an orgasm as a poor man's epiphany?"

I'm saying uh-huh, yes, really. I keep asking him some version of the question What is the sex *about*?

"A complete moment of carnal, pure . . . moment. It's heady stuff. Say your dad was out one night and got shoved

onto the dance floor at Studio 54. He was a disco bunny
hanging out with musicians and decorators and people with
money. I can still see him—silk shirt unbuttoned down just
far enough, he's having a good hair day. He has all the
right connections. What could be better? Your dad was not
an unsophisticated man, but New York is still gonna bring
out your gee-whiz.

"Me, I still go economy class. Not nearly as much fun
as the wretched excess of your father's heyday. Last night
I drank about a million beers, smoked a ton of dope. I'm
blotto, dancing. You need a little cocaine to complicate
things if you've done it a million times. Yeah, you want the
feeling of having been purely and completely outside yourself. Well, I was in the groove, and these thoughts bolt in:
my dad is a Pentecostal minister. I believe Jesus died on
the Cross. What does that have to do with anything? It's 4
a.m. and I'm riding my bike home in the freezing cold,
stoned out of my mind, and I'm thinking, Was I just dancing
with Satan?

"Susan, I know what your father went through. His
has sadly been the fundamental drama of my last ten years.
If you come from our world and you're a homosexual, you
can't be your parents' child. You can't be a Christian (or
can you?). Think about it. Potentially I would be doomed
to the bottom rung of hell.

"My father and I always had this inside joke he thought
was funny. Unlike your father, mine hated appearances,
any smack of vanity. He called me Narcissus. Any time he
caught me fussing with my hair or glancing in the mirror,
he would sing a little song: *There's this certain yellow flower*
. . . The flower was forsythia and somehow that rhymed for

him with Narcissus. He would sing in a high-pitched voice
to let me know he'd caught me primping.

"For all my misbehavior, I feel very fortunate to have
the leisure to reevaluate why I've made the choices I have
these past several years. To be healthy in 1993 with all the
screwing around I've done, I've gotten away with a lot. I'm
sorry your father wasn't so fortunate. The weird thing about
AIDS is how it has demystified homosexuality in some ways.
You think less about what's bad for your soul and more
about what's bad for your body. I really don't think that God
cares whether or not I'm sucking Gordon's dick. Ultimately
what could be better than that, Susan?"

In the rhetorical delay that follows his question I think
of a few things I decide not to mention.

"Don't tell me," he says. "Looking into your little girl's
eyes."

The woman with the taper cut hands the phone to the
woman with the pure white trimmed bangs. Or for all I
know, they may appear entirely changed by now. "Oh yes,
we remember your father well," she says. "Here, talk with
Sal. I'm running to the market."

"You're his oldest daughter?" Sal asks. I can hear her
voice, searching backwards to a mental image that fits the
past. I've thought of two reasons I could mention (in case
she asks) why I've called after all these years. First to find
out about the ownership of the Henshaw paintings and
drawings, a few of which I have hanging in my house.
"They're mine," she says. "They've always been mine and
I can prove it. I have the papers. Where are they? Do you
have the little girl in the red dress?"

"I have some of the pastels and the drawings." I tell her quickly what happened to the others. "I wasn't sure whether or not my father had ever paid you for them. My mother was cleaning out an old drawer and found your number, so I thought I'd get in touch."

"Well, he paid me. Twice. And both times the checks bounced. You mean they're gone? Why didn't he get those back to me if he couldn't sell them? I wish he'd been more honest with me. How is he and the rest of your family? It's been quite a long time, hasn't it?" Her accent sounds mildly Southern, with a pleasing laughter softening the edges of her adamance. I'm not sure if she's joking or angry.

"My father died ten years ago." Didn't she know this?

"Was it AIDS-related?" she asks.

This was my second reason for calling, and the first time in all these years that anyone has even hinted that they knew my father as a homosexual without my asking.

"Yes, it was AIDS. I think we all wish he'd been more honest."

"Your mother was the one he lied to, not you. He raised some good kids. That's not true that he lied to you. It's none of your damn business what your father did in the bed-room."

"His behavior had an effect on all our lives, don't you think?" I try to phrase it mildly. "His fear of being found out . . ." She is easy to talk with, pushy as I push back. The swift rhythm to our banter belies the stakes our conversation holds for each of us.

"Well, he wasn't afraid of sex, you oughta know. He had a helluva good time doing it."

Had she surmised or witnessed this? Had he spoken freely with her? "When you knew him was he active in some sort of a gay community in Cleveland? Is that how you met him?"

"I don't know where we met. I'm not a gossip. I wouldn't tell Joe Blow's secrets. He was already going to New York by the time we met, wanting to be discreet and to protect your mother. He recognized in me my talent as an artist. Most gay people are extremely talented. God gives us this little extra piece of our brain that is artistic—and he saw that in me. Yes, he was in the design business. Don't think that he lied to you, because he didn't."

"Did he say anything to you about protecting his identity; you know, don't mention seeing me here to my family, or anything?"

"It was unnecessary that we talk about it. It wasn't a decision on his part; oh good Lord, no. He was born that way. It takes one to know one. God loves us all or He wouldn't have made so many of us. So we're all right. Sweet and nice and wonderful. If he promised things that didn't occur, he can't be condemned for that, not in the first day. Not in the last. There's not a God's world thing we can do about it.

"I was never unhappy being myself like he was. I was disappointed that I was, of course, at first. Who the hell wants to be different? If you don't have the tendency you can't be straight, just like you can't be gay if you're not."

"How did you know?"

"How did *you* know? Do you remember your first sexual experience? Did you tell your parents about it? You can tell by your dreams. Your dreams tell you who you really are. Do you dream about the boys or about the girls?"

"Then why do you think my father married and had a family? Why did he stay married?" I'm asking her to speculate about a different kind of life than the one she's evidently chosen of long-term monogamy. I'm asking as though she is an expert on my father's life, which she isn't.

"To try to conform. To Christianize. We were all taught it is a sin. It isn't—if you can't figure that out by now. Homosexuals are truer than most people are to each other. Esther and I have been true blue to each other for forty or fifty years. The young ones haven't made up their minds yet and they shouldn't. So many of them end up suicides. But we have been married and faithful to one person much longer than most of you have.

"I have to run now," she says. "We're having ten people over for dinner. If you ever get to Miami come and stay in our guest house. We can talk for longer. I'll help however I can. Some of my best friends are straight." She chuckles again and gives me her address so that I can send the drawings.

"It was the first death from AIDS that we had come into contact with," the pastor of the last church he attended tells me. He knows my name when I introduce myself and gently inquires about my mother and sisters. He knows that Nathan is dead. "So many times I've wondered about your family," he says. "I had many conversations with your dad. We had begun to use him in our music ministry because we saw how talented he was and how much he had to contribute. At first he came with different friends, but eventually he was by himself. He told me he was making a change in his life—he was trying to come out of his homosexual lifestyle. When he went to the altar for prayer, he would openly weep, confessing. In my coming to know Don he was repeatedly remorseful. He knew he had wronged your mother and recognized that what he had given up was irreplaceable.

"He had just begun to come down with symptoms. We thought it was bronchitis. He kept coughing. We went on the road with a musical group from the church for which your dad was the accompanist. I was his roommate for that tour. We had many conversations during that time about your family and his struggle. His deterioration was extremely rapid. You will want to talk with a woman in our church who took care of your father those last days."

"Near the end they experimented on your father as though he were a guinea pig," Shirley tells me. She is a woman who understands pain, having lived with it herself. She cannot forget, by her own testimony, that when she was dying Jesus gave His life for her. So she finds the ravaged and helps, simply, whatever pain or lack she is given to assuage. "They did spinal taps and bone marrow extractions, bronchoscopies and T-cell counts. They tried chemotherapy and every other treatment they could dream up."

"This will hurt, I told him. You can hang on to my arm and squeeze as hard as you need to. He was trying to be upbeat that day, even though he felt lousy. The doctors stuck this long needle into his spine—I'm saying, Grab on, grab on. Go ahead and yell—and he just sat there like a statue, looking straight ahead. He didn't make a sound."

"Did he talk to you at all about being gay?" I ask.

"The only thing we ever really talked about was his family. You children were the delight of his life. Nathan left him a card at the hospital one time. When I read it to him, tears just streamed down his face. He sensed a spirit of forgiveness. I didn't pry a lot, though I knew two and two. I tried to help him as much as I could. I didn't have a single doubt about God's love for him."

Shirley met my father one Sunday morning in October of 1982 at the Lambs' Manhattan Church of the Nazarene. He had been playing for the morning services and directing the choir. When the pastor invited people to come forward for prayer after the service, Shirley had followed him down the aisle. She could see the silver-dollar lesions. He was having surgery the next day. "Do you mind if I come and visit you?" she said.

"When he got out of the hospital I brought him here to recover. I went down to help him move his things. The whole homosexual community was in a panic. We didn't know how it spread. I disinfected everything he touched from the start, washed his clothes separately. Sweat is body fluid; I cleaned under my fingernails. I just didn't know. You wouldn't believe how everyone goes away when you have AIDS."

I think of the recently celebrated cases in which valiant partners have fashioned a common mythology out of their shared suffering. But ask in the free clinics and overcrowded destitution wards about men who fed their disease into blood banks for a meal, men whose early AIDS was shackled with such a stigma that their bedsides were abandoned early and their bodies never claimed. The last six months of his life Shirley let my father live in the spare bedroom of her apartment. She stocked a separate shelf in her refrigerator with the food she'd buy him each week, asking what he thought would taste good. She took over the care that my mother had always imagined she would administer to her husband when they were old and he needed her most, that tender serving a life partner would not easily relinquish if someone else stepped in.

During the nights he was very restless. When Shirley wasn't traveling with her job she could hear him pacing long before morning.

She had been away and came home one evening as my father was getting out of the shower. "There he stood in his towel in the hallway, bald as a cue ball and without his beard. It was the chemo. I just laughed out loud. 'You look very funny,' I said. His hair had all washed down the drain. 'Better get dressed, we're gonna go get you some hair.' I took him up to Fifty-seventh Street and bought him a good-quality wig, and then we went and had it cut on his head so that it looked exactly like his own hair. We told the choir on Sunday that he'd shaved his beard."

When she was in town she went to the hospital every day and read to him. He asked to hear certain passages of Scripture; the Psalms especially comforted him. She would suggest from time to time that she call his family. "Wouldn't they like to know how you're doing?" But he was insistent that they wouldn't want to see him. It would be a bother. He would hoard the hurt as though the ones who loved him were too weak or too condemning. He had done them an injustice they couldn't be expected to forgive.

A week or two before he died, they moved him to a hospital room with another patient who shared his symptoms, and hung a warning sign on the door. They asked Shirley to wear gloves and a mask and to be tested for the disease. "If it's in the air," she said, "I've got it. That's the only way I could have caught what he's got." The doctors hadn't known what her relationship to my father was or why she showed such care.

She was driving the young man from the next bed to the train station—he was heading home to his parents' house—when my father died. That morning he had been too weak to open his eyes. "The Lord is my Shepherd," she had read, quietly. Those words seemed to comfort him most. "I shall not want."

Shirley makes a point of assuring me that though his was an agonizing death my father died at peace with his Maker. More than her confidence in my father's place in heaven, her humble kindness toward him both consoles and convicts me. The savage deterioration of body and mind—couldn't I have seen that and put aside whatever grudge I nursed? Talking with her (has it really been ten years?) I begin to feel my heart breaking for my father for the very first time. This is what I could have offered him—in her face, in the generosity of her touch, my father had been able to observe the most innocent and natural sorrow, that of bereavement. Not because she revered him as I had, I remember now—though barely knowing him at all she could tell he was not merely a weak man—not because she understood the treatment or reason for his disease, but because she saw that he was dying and remembered an even greater compassion that had been offered her.

"And then there was the problem of finding a funeral home that would accept the body. No undertaker wanted the risk of poking around with AIDS." Their pastor helped her find a place on the Lower East Side. She gave them his navy suit and his wedding ring. "When we went to see the body it looked nothing like Don. His face was all bloated and rouged. They had put his wig on backwards." Knowing he wouldn't like that, she reached down into the casket and lifted up his head with one hand while with the other she twisted his hair on frontward.

I always thought that if I had the chance I would lavish on my father the fallout of his hypocrisy—Hold this, Mystery Man—so he wouldn't get away with it, the way the dead do. All the shame we felt even in front of each other, the pretense each of us inherited that we've begun to peel away. We have lives underneath it all other than the ones we thought we'd lived.

That was our biggest problem. The way we loved who we thought he was kept stealing our appetite for the truth. We missed his image like crazy. In the hospital I'd held a mirror up for him so that he could comb his hair, and he had flinched. That's not you, I tried to console him, you are.

When my mother asked him directly before he died if he'd had any homosexual encounters, I can sympathize with his lying. It's hard to tell the truth in front of people whose lives we think depend on illusions. Maybe what he tried to do was to say who he was in the extreme diction of the body's speech.

He thought it would be over with his death, the whole story. He did not account for Nathan's loss, and Abigail's reeling out over the deep end like live bait, and Anne's ingrained mistrust that a man could ever prefer her to another man. He didn't play out his widow's long nights. I had meant to grab him and shake him. But how stooped he looked. Did I really think I could impress our hurts on him more deeply than his self-recrimination had? Did I think he'd lost his life for nothing?

> *. . . let their blood come*
> *To beg for us, a discreet patience*
> *Of death, or of worse life: for oh, to some*
> *Not to be martyrs is a martyrdom.*
>
> —JOHN DONNE

10 /

*D*uring those first few years, after our knowledge of our losses, our inability to mend devoured us: we must have let it. Sudden onslaughts of blankness set in, or guilt for thinking of anything but the dead. Or a wrenching shame at our own distress (who could listen so patiently) gripped us and heaved us from rooms in the middle of sentences or meals. We circled our remains like birds of prey. I wanted to think of us as bullfinches, linnets, siskins, grosbeaks, yellowhammers, nightingales, but bodiless, from further in. What harm could come to such birds as grace us with strains of song? A grain head for nourishment, an insect caught in flight. Although, I've learned that canaries, unless they're given scraped raw meat in the spring at brooding time, will pull out their feathers and nibble the ends of them, so ravenous are they for the taste of flesh.

I leaned my forehead on the cool downstairs window against which half a dozen birds would knock themselves silly. Why should we not open the sashes of this cloistral house? They may have flown from a great distance to taste the seeds of our lament. They may have been here all along, whirring like the bony parts of grasshoppers.

Standing on the wooden footbridge too near the female barnswallow's nest, I watched her swoop and dive to divert me. Her iridescent blue wings, her golden belly plunging and frantic, flailed a mad-show, feigning herself lame-winged, through loops of despair. Ten shades of feather turned prismatic in the light. When I slept, dreams of her rustled the dream's air. A bird like that, I thought, effectual and gorgeous, free in the unrestricted air, unlike, day after day, the berserk lurch of my mind along the narrow track of its preoccupations. What loss was given I was anxious to match. You can hear it in my hushed voice—over again, I whisper the unconvincing supplication of survivors, and over: *Take me first, take me.*

After paying the last of my father's debts and taking care of her son's funeral expenses, my mother moved to Chicago. She was finding her way around the city shops and conveniences, work serving as her therapy. She hadn't the time a widow friend of hers had taken to travel alone and grieve. So she went through the necessary motions distractedly, half-conscious, coping. Leaving the Jersey Shore, she returned to her familiar Midwest. Chicago was closer to where the rest of the family lived. Her mother still ran the GOP newspaper in a small Indiana county seat. Mom would earn a living for herself and her two teenage daughters. She would furnish her apartment slowly, as income allowed, with other families' castoffs. A new life would begin, eventually, far from the wreckage of the last.

I was in Chicago too, teaching at a private college, with a second child on the way. Nine o'clock at night, after my last student had turned in his exam, I called home. The babysitter rushed to read the telephone message just as she had written it down: "An emergency with your mother. Abigail says she thinks everything will be okay. You can call Grant Hospital." From the emergency room, where my middle sister had been keeping vigil, she gave me an account of the accident in her stony voice. A valet parking attendant in front of the apartment where my mother lived had accidentally floored the accelerator of the car he was parking.

"We don't know if the pedal jammed or if he was stoned," Abi says. "Mom was crossing the street and was thrown up onto the hood and windshield of the car." I sink to the floor of my office, trying to listen. "What cut her up was that when the driver swerved to avoid a car he plowed right through a chain-link fence. Her legs went through the fence with the front of the car and the rest of her body was crushed against the window."

"Is she conscious?" I ask. By now my first reaction isn't denial but credulity. It must be so. We have come to expect, no, to deserve, the worst.

"An ambulance came right away. There were witnesses. I think she was in and out of her head, kinda. If you can get here in the morning . . . she'll be pretty groggy tonight, I guess."

My mother is badly scraped and bruised. The tendons in one ankle are torn, and all the way up her legs the barbs of the fence have dug into her flesh. She wakes in pain, fretting about the scars. The "miracle" of no broken bones on which the nurses keep remarking is small consolation. I ask how she is feeling again and again. It is her practiced cheer letting down these days, stiffening across her mouth, that has alarmed me. The owners of the restaurant in her apartment building whose valet had been driving the run-away car have already called and sent flowers by the time I weave my way through the morning traffic. I tell their lawyer we will call him back. Sitting by the window in a wheelchair when I walk into the room, my mother grimaces with the slight movement of her head and shoulders as she greets me. Speaking of her last weeks of settling in, she mentions Nathan, work, her memory lapses, wanting to marry again soon. "What is this about?" she asks, confused, her thoughts a puzzle of wire and skin. "What will be next?" She is wailing now in the gulpless high-pitched voice she has grown accustomed to breaking into, her after-death voice. The helpless, helpless vein of noise before word-lessness.

We sit very still. I have brought the morning paper and read to her, to muffle the hospital's medicated quiet, about the Pope's visit to the lepers and to the nursing home where more than half the residents burned to death in a fire. My mother isn't listening. An ambulance speeds past her street-level window. A nurse wafts into the room with the high-pitched stench of rubbing alcohol and urine trailing her.

"You shouldn't read what you can't change," my mother says, never one for world hurt. The medicine is making her words flat with drowsiness.

She must have needed some air last evening. She looked across at the statue of Shakespeare in the park, or up at the limestone gargoyles on the building's façade. Across the street from her building was an entrance to the narrow lagoon where the crew team from a nearby university daily kept its segmented rhythm going; their muscular strain like her son's, their unruly hair. Their oars sent a signal undecipherable to her. What of their gleaming shoulders? She wishes someone would help her pay her rent. She thinks she is not hungry yet, though it's after six. The doorman is throwing his hat toward the car, which is picking up speed, isn't it? The thud of her torso, head on, and the wild jumble of her white legs and arms tearing the dusk. She didn't even hear . . . swiftly into the oncoming traffic over the curb. She feels all at once the scrape of the diamond-weave metal, fractured by the impact and stripping her flesh and muscle into thick strands, all the way up; she is alive, then nothing.

What was happening to us, my mother and sisters and me? This undignified grieving, our unrelenting powerlessness to stop feeding ourselves into the gaping mouth of more, more. As if we had found the purpose, the moral necessity for suffering, we surrendered voluntarily, or would have if asked, but there were no torturers. No famished lions, no bone-splintering rack—oh, for the flamboyance of captivity. Trouble made our plans. We ached without its fresh diversions.

There was nothing that qualified our suffering for martyrdom, though we compared our predicaments to those of
Joan of Arc or Electra ("Inside my body, I am feeding a
vulture!"), to Salvadoran women on the ten o'clock news,
to Perpetua, who in her own apocalyptic hand recorded
tortures she lived through and visions of deliverance. We
did not deserve the title of martyr, of course, though we
were heartily pitied, and at first we pitied ourselves as such.

Those first years we lived in a kind of stupor: days of
the most prolix and undisturbed vacancies. One season we
spent looking for signs of the next. The mockingbird pon-
tificated on the shadows cast by the sun, on reflections in
stagnant waters. The sparrow tensed on the wire. Jaybird,
Heart-numb. All but our distress remained unfinished. I
put out with the energy of a band of maniacs. Put out, I
said, I did not get back; or put on, that is what it must have
been. Whenever we needed to go out in public we wore a
sort of pert wellness that worked if no one in our hearing
touched on any topic having to do with home. Anything
dreadful could have been about to happen; we did not
recoil.

Mothers of the missing in war, orphaned children, the
martyrs knew us when we met them on the street—Hunger,
Disease, Pain, Affliction—mentally greeting them as if with
misery's secret handshake. It was their lives I found myself
seeking in old newspapers and library stacks, flood records,
accident reports, journals the survivors kept, the inadvert-
ently aggrandized stories of eyewitnesses, recorded, it
seemed to me, for others' consolation. There are the *pas-
siones'* gruesome deaths to sort through, the comparatively
milder afflictions suffered at the hands of Nero and Flavian.
I read histories of the high-styled barbarisms of Domitian,

transcriptions of predetermined trials, reviving one of my less suitable childhood preoccupations.

As a child I had seen the early victims of their own clear faith in Foxe's *Book of Christian Martyrs*, which we had a copy of in our church library. Sunday mornings after the service, while the parents commiserated and the other children played games on the front stairs, I would open the book's leather covers to the etchings placed between the written accounts of torture and death. There on the broken-edged pages, like a sanctified peep show, the martyrs' naked bodies writhed in the fire or stretched uncovered on the rack until their limbs split and their blood spattered the witnesses. No genital or emotional detail had been spared. Eyes toward heaven, some sang out the hymns we had just sung; some, open-mouthed, prayed for their executioners' souls. I ranked the agonies in order of my preference: flagellation, impalement, scalding, tigers, crucifixion.

We took our trials—they supplied us with a sense of destiny—too seriously, bearing our grief like an affront, lashing out at others for their inferior woes. Though I had (and *still have*) a sense as I went of being watched over, less delivered than simply seen by God. No birds plucked out our eyes. The flames have died down.

The second anniversary of my brother's death fell on the day of Anne's high-school graduation. She had just ended a run of Thornton Wilder's *Our Town* at the private city school she'd been attending, known for its performing arts. Her grades were good; she had adapted to a new city quickly and had a lot of friends. She had been courted by all the television networks for roles in their soap operas, and had been flying back and forth to New York for screen tests during and around finals week.

Abigail, who had graduated two years earlier, had completed only a semester of college. She had rushed through junior and senior years in Ocean City so that she and Nathan (who was one year older) could be freshmen at Wheaton together. It was the beginning of the summer before they were to drive to orientation that she had gone to identify Nathan's body at the morgue after the crash. Alone on campus, her father and brother freshly buried, Abigail broke a few of the rules. The "pledge," Wheaton students call it—no smoking, no drinking or drugs, no sex: enrollees sign their names to it before they are admitted. The dean of women didn't issue any warning. Within three months Abigail was asked to leave and not invited back. There was no explaining to the authorities, no request for lenience given the situation. What would be her excuse? It was too soon after the deaths and the cause of the deaths for any of us to say out loud what we knew. The pretense of a family intact to which she would return had been easier, and would always be, we assumed. Others didn't need to know.

The young man involved, a senior, played on the varsity football team. His boast to supposed friends had snared them. His was not a first offense, nor was it his first time to be caught after hours in the freshman women's dorm, but he was permitted to finish his degree after a quarter's reformation.

So Abigail had temporarily moved in with my mother. She had taken a job at a stylish men's clothier in a fashionable part of the city, coordinating shirts and ties. She could hold pins in her mouth and hem trousers. She could date the customers when work ended and found someone in a short time who offered her a place to live. Bobby sold advertising for a local Spanish-language radio station. He got free tickets to events they rode to on his Harley. The strain that his children and estranged wife placed on their developing relationship kept getting in the way. Abigail wrote down the symptoms she could remember from TV. Loss of appetite, insomnia, indifference to sex, recurring thoughts of suicide, lack of motivation. She couldn't remember the other three; they didn't apply to her. Neither did suicide, actually, though she had imagined herself jumping from an airplane without a parachute. "If five or more of these eight symptoms apply to you," the soothing voice said, "see a doctor. You are probably suffering from depression." Now that she thought about it, though it was a thousand miles away, yes, she could picture wearing her full-length wool coat into the ocean.

Because none of the family approved of Abigail's arrangements with Bobby, though he seemed to be a friendly-enough man, or because of the white powder my mother discovered in her purse (not snooping, but having mislaid her keys), because we had no idea what to say to one another amid our foundational ruins, she lost touch with the rest of us more and more, or we lost her. From her perspective the whole universe must have been mined with conspiracy: I could hear her thinking, *You must have told them or they wouldn't have known.*

But here she was on Anne's graduation day, on the second anniversary of our brother's loss. She chose a seat in the middle of the auditorium. None of us had seen her come in. She hadn't called. After the scholarships had been awarded, the principal read through the list of seniors' names alphabetically. With the parade of gowns through the F's and G's and then at H, "Anne Heche," he said into the microphone.

Abigail, in a tight blue-leather halter dress, stood up, cupped her hands around her mouth, and shouted, "Is it signed, Anne? Make sure it's signed." That was evidently what she'd come for. She would do her family duty and violate it. Plowing her way across the feet and knees of snickerers out to the edge of her row, she sauntered up the aisle toward the back doors, letting their closing bang echo through the dim auditorium. Anne stood still for a moment, hearing the familiar voice but not able to see its source. In practiced form, without a hint of awkwardness, she delivered a graceful bow, first to the rest of her class, seated in the front rows, then to the larger audience, before crossing the stage to accept the scrolled diploma and a pale, coral-colored rose.

By the third year I had two children and needed to snap out of it. Grief alone felt stagy, but not as artificial as joy. Wasn't I more susceptible feeling than not feeling, to getting sucked back in? Enough of visions and waking dread. I wanted to define my days by something other than the fallout of our family woes. While the babies had napped through to the early evening, I had wandered from task to task, and still they slept—a reprieve from the routine, but disconcerting.

There was tomorrow's lecture to prepare on the seventeenth-century Spanish school of painters. I had slides to pull and coordinate with my talk. Think of it, the entire court of Philip IV and everyone in *Las Meniñas* dead by now. I imagined the dwarf expiring, perhaps of natural causes, perhaps quitting the palace service and the side of the Infanta Margarita not knowing why, and in a dress especially fitting wandering one day soon after the portrait was completed toward the river, where she lay down and stopped breathing. It would have been the palace dog, a docile mutt Velázquez may have kicked, that found her that same evening with her eyes wide open, frowning. Tangled in her hair, an oriole that had fluttered deliriously to free himself lay settled in a nest close to her ear. Every image funereal, I knew what I was leaving out but could not yet restore the picture.

I checked the children's breathing one more time and let them rest. From the back porch it was easy to feel winter following fall. Dusk came earlier and a dense wind strewed humidity and unraked leaves. Nothing could quench my thirst that night, or clear the thickness that sloughed from the weather into my throat. If the deaths had been ordinary—what would that be like, not to have situations and words between us that stank of regret?

Abigail's boyfriend had driven her to the airport to collect me the day after our brother died. The man stood some distance back from our embrace. We both must have wondered what to say to the other, and said that—I don't remember any words. As we walked the airport's wide, fuel-smelling passages to the parking lot, we stopped occasionally, just stopped and stood there. The man hurried ahead to open doors. He helped us into his vintage yellow Cadillac and drove us home.

My family had found a tiny flat upstairs from a real-estate office, with a living room about ten feet wide, a galley kitchen behind, and three minuscule bedrooms off to one side. My mother was working outside the home, for the first time in twenty-five years, as a secretary at a brokerage firm. She was seeing "someone." The usual off-balance girlish lilt to her voice when she called to tell me about Nathan had had the wind knocked out of it.

The highway's drone, as we drove, the blaring sunny day, the garish beach town billboards amplified the wreck. On June 5 the resort was cranking at its early summer tilt. When I climbed the outside stairway to the front door, all I wanted to do was punish my mother. That impulse had outstripped (or preceded) my grief. The hurl of my father's neglect had been compounded by her absence. She was in New York with Someone that night; for hours no one knew where to reach her. The children were to keep an eye on each other. Abigail stayed out all night. Anne was babysitting late and came home to an empty apartment. Nathan, between two and four in the morning, on a curved road without lights, overtired—where was she?—wrapped his car around a tree.

Abi stayed in the air-conditioned car as I found my way up the unfamiliar stairs and knocked. It wasn't my house. No answer. I walked in and heard some muffled noises coming from the back room. Anne had gone to the neighbors' to let them know what was going on, her note said. I made my way through the dark hall-like front room to the corner bedroom, where my mother lay curled under the blankets on her bed. She shook with half-audible, dry noise. I barely recognized her. Her face looked almost gray and her hair was crushed against one cheek as she raised her head slowly, then weakly let it fall.

"I hope it was worth it," I said.

For the time it took me to say that she lay perfectly frozen, and then she convulsed horribly, soundlessly. What syllables were there? She pulled her knees up under her body to bury her head more deeply.

I was remembering this the night of the dense wind, and the uninterrupted breath of the children. My beautiful, tenderhearted mother. That was all I said to her. Then I walked into my brother's room and stood looking into his closet at his shirts and shoes. Standing there I did not weigh the magnitude of my mother's experience on a different scale than mine: she had lost a husband and son. I, from some remove, was trying to get back my brother.

You hear that it will happen all at once. Trouble consolidates so that by the fourth or fifth round the connections between act and consequence, the actual effects, no longer register. Break your back, and what is a cloudy day? You learn to calibrate degrees of need. You nurture what you can, not of yourself, necessarily, but of the visible world. Not because life is dear (your own family is a testimony to its easy dissipation) but so as to reestablish a routine. Vapidly you tidy your surroundings—fold the sheets again corner to corner, the towels. Place them squarely on the newly papered shelves where they belong. Discard any unmatched socks, emotionlessly. For the others: think of the children.

There are small animals to bury, slain mysteriously in the yard. And birds to rescue and feed equal parts of boiled potato and egg yolk crumb. A hen robin brooding in the cottonwood drops a mouthful to her yawning chicks (and to the catbird's offspring nearly her size) and they survive, but not our broken-winged vireo in the rag box.

Elliot, my three-year-old, runs into the kitchen pant-

ing. "Mom, I saw a giant bird kill a rabbit. Come see!" A
crow is feeding on a rabbit all right, and suddenly the wild
animal's carcass qualifies it for our domestic protectorate.
I grab my jacket and close the door behind me. The rabbit
is freshly dead. Its body is intact but for a leg torn off and
some tufts of fur the birds have plucked from its belly. The
crow lifts off with a clean white fragment of bone. We are
both hesitant to lean over and touch it. Tired of obligatory
sympathy, we don't know what to say. Elliot looks at me
and smiles, and I start to laugh, then he laughs. We look
at each other, laughing uncontrollably, the way I laughed
at my great-aunt's funeral when I was seven and had to be
excused from the parlor. The way you laugh in church when
someone belches loudly—silly rabbit. It is not conceivable
that we could both be laughing about the same thing. I am
twenty-seven and the mother; he is the three-year-old son.
It's not funny. We stop laughing. Better to say, I'll get a
shovel; we can bury it. "Why not leave it for the birds?"
Elliot asks, poking with a stick between the stiffening hind
legs, peering into the small bleak crater where, a few minutes before, an eye had been.

My grandmother's voice on the other end of the line
kept cracking. "Have you heard from your mother?" She
is part sniffling, part smothering herself with her handkerchief. I had been sleeping so I missed what she was saying
the first time. "Did your mother call you?" she asks again.
I worry that my mother has had a relapse; her legs had
been healing so well since her accident. She was walking
without her cane from room to room. Usually she waits
until after seven to check in with me, in case the babies
sleep late. "No?" my grandmother says as I run through

all the possibilities. "Well, down here on the news they're showing pictures of her apartment building burning."

Now I am thinking, This has gone too far. A fire, don't tell me. I reassure my grandmother through my pre-dawn grog that the cement floors of the Belden Stratford are eighteen inches thick. Maybe the curtains will go up in smoke, maybe the Chinese laundry in the back has turned out its last ironed shirt. The restaurant could have set fire to its leftovers. Really, this must be a hoax. I promise to call her back when I know more and hang up the phone serenely confident, for no reason, in the building's long history, in its well-structured fire escapes. I trust the fire department's record of competence with my mother's and sisters' lives. I believe, pulling on my jeans, that whatever happens now will not happen to us. We are saturated with eventfulness. Strike any epilogue from the record. Enough is enough. The world is going to have to play its petty tragedies on other people's stages.

Within the hour my phone rings: it's my mother. They are back in the building and safe, she says, assuming I have heard the news. An iron's cord went haywire in the laundry. No one hurt. Anne was perturbed to have been awakened so early; you can imagine. They've been standing across the street in the park for two hours and are frozen stiff. I picture them, in the din of the fire alarm, dashing into clothes and dabbing on makeup, the smoke exhaling into the lobby as they make themselves presentable for the firemen.

Yesterday, despite the ornery wind, I tried to rake the leaves into piles. I took shallow breaths. My mother's dream filled the air. The night before, she had walked into the living room of their first house in Shaker Heights. Under the small window with the silver-encased bottle of aqua-marine water on the sill stood the old green-and-blue chair. She could count the grapes on the fabric print; the air of the dream and her vision of the room were that clear. The down pillows of the long blue sofa lay strewn about the floor. She would have to fluff them and put them back in place. And then Don was there picking up the pillows and arranging them, as he always did, carefully, just right. You must not sit on the sofa or your body will leave an imprint.

"I felt so whole, seeing him," my mother said. "He was actually truly alive again, and I thought in the dream, *This is not a dream, it's really happening this time.* I was so happy we would be able to talk together. He would straighten up the room. I would be married to him again, and that was who I wanted to be, his wife."

"That's really how you felt?"

"I was completely happy. I saw him and couldn't wait to talk with him. Finally, I thought, he's back. We'll be able to clear this whole thing up. So we sat down together on the couch, and when I looked over at him it wasn't Don at all, it was a waitress. She was wearing a little blue dress with a white apron. It was Don, but he was a waitress."

All these leaves gusting from their piles as I rake them. The surfeit of wind against my chest. In the blank trees linger birds that devour and birds that sing, birds of color, weightless, black birds. There are evidently years for each of us, stretches of disaster balanced, as we turn from them, by blessing. Turning is not flying. It cannot be conducted at a uniform pace: left wing, right wing. I remind myself not to begrudge time to anyone returning.

"Fall is upon us, the melancholy time of year," my grandmother writes. "I am extremely susceptible. Drop a line when you can." The ruckus of geese circling the pond for their evening feed, landing asquawk, carried on late into the night as I stirred the last leaves into the fire. By midnight the sparks and stars were distinguishable only by the paler color from the distance and the golden orange up close. The white egrets had gone south, but the heron was still here. I'd seen only the one flying low over the pond, just high enough to clear the trees.

"Father," said I, "do you see this vase here, for example, or water pot or whatever?"

"Yes, I do," said he.

And I told him: "Could it be called by any other name than what it is?"

And he said: "No."

"Well, so too I cannot be called anything other than what I am."

       —PERPETUA OF AFRICA, *late second century*
           (translated by Herbert Musurillo)

11   /   Sunday morning, late November, the chill rose from the frost-clenched ground into the air just on schedule: those crisp days before life burrows into its winter lairs. Cold but bright. I tried to remember how soon the first snow came last year and a freeze took hold of the season. That morning I had opted to stay home alone. Not feeling well, I must have told Judson. Another long week.

    I can smell that morning and feel the dampness that leeched through the stitching of my boots as I walked down the hill in front of our house to the edge of the pond. There was a fallen tree to sit on. The cattails had exploded their velvet grenades and the yellow-flag iris sported thumb-sized pods. Leafless strands of willow reflected on the water's skin. Judson and I usually met on Sunday mornings with a group of friends to talk about our lives. We devoted each week to a different person in the group. At the end of the session one of us would present in writing the topic for next week's discussion—a pressing decision, family trouble, an area of growth and what that meant . . . that week in November was Judson's.

"I am afraid of intimacy (to some extent)," he had written on the page we passed around the table, "especially with those closest to me: my wife, closest friends, parents. I feel that maybe I should be less comfortable and more vulnerable in my relationships." General but daring.

Together we would look for the qualities he exhibited that blocked love coming and going. He would blame himself, as we suggested ways to release emotion, fear. We would encourage him with our own stories, or the group would; I would try to keep quiet and out of the way of his worry. What could they tell him that he hadn't already perfected? If I were there I would listen to their take on his motives and behavior—weren't we always able to make small progress together and to care?—concealing from them some key pieces that would make the puzzle of his apprehension fit. He would agree to go back to those relationships and try in new ways. "More of a good thing!" someone would laugh.

I would go with him and fake it, again, or I would stay home. Afraid of me? I wasn't feeling my best, that much was true. He could get more out of the session if I wasn't present. Since his issue involved me, I might be an inhibitor, I said. I'm not feeling well. I'll just stay home. With the person I most loved I was still pretending, and was sick of it.

Since I was a little girl I have wanted to be the same as myself all the way through. Layer upon layer; aligned, I called it. This ideal took different forms: one time the vision of transparency; another, recognizing I could not be seen through like an insect wing, I envisioned the incidents of my life as a set of matched beads strung on an unbreakably thin floss of truth. Or I simply longed for one person to listen to the whole story, bead by bead, all the way to the knot. This is a lot to hope for: for another to want to know you that well. It would only be fair, naturally, if I agreed to reciprocate, and I was willing. There were those who shared my hope with great enthusiasm, could in fact articulate their longing better than I. Join me, I would say. I do not want to be invisible; I want to be known all the way in.

But though this has been my rather abstract and compensatory life principle, I am not adept at aligning my behavior with my ambition. From an early age I was a liar. Not only would I lie to protect myself from punishment (Did you brush your teeth? Yes, I did), I would make up untruths on the playground, boasting of my family's ancestry and inheritance of royal treasures or of my own physical or mental prowess. Not only a bull's-eye, my shot knocked the other arrows off the target. Not only could I spell, I could invent new words. In my pocket burned a jewel of eighty carats; wrapped in silk was a watch that told eternal time. Impossible, let me see. I couldn't show you. It would burn the very sockets of your eyes. Would not.

Would so. Prove it. My rivals were fellow woodsmen and sharpshooters, those who could tie strong knots, weaving and unraveling tapestries of like magnitude. We could make ourselves up as we went along.

At first no one believed me and I knew it. On Sunday nights until I was at least ten (not every week) my parents spanked me for my week's worth of lies, until I cried so hard I would lose my breath. Eventually I learned how to simulate breath loss so they'd stop before the welts rose. I practiced on the gullible until, satisfied that even skeptics would not doubt, I told the one about my father's performance at Carnegie Hall. He was that talented, and when the other children heard him play they imagined him on a gilded proscenium with the ebony grand piano lid propped all the way open, just as I had described it, so that the sound could reach the uppermost balcony, where I sat as he rehearsed. I wanted him to be as good in their minds as he seemed to me. I knew that if I could have seen him as he was meant to be, this is how he would have appeared.

My father had a talent for the way things sounded and the way things looked. He could make the circle of us in our folding chairs that we'd set up for evening church sound like a choir of angels. From the piano bench he could both play the accompaniment and keep the time like a skilled conductor.

"Will you teach me how to do that?" I asked him another Sunday morning a long time ago as I was watching him tie his tie.

"In four/four time you start at the top, drop your hand straight down, then raise it at an angle to the left, that's it, straight past the center bar to the right as far as you went left, then up at an angle back to your starting point." I could see the same crooked butterfly in the air that he made when I traced my hand along the imaginary lines he told me to. I could curve the invisible figure like a crazy eight; I could make the wings' edge crisp with march time.

That morning my father was teaching the eight-to-ten-year-old Sunday-school class. The parents rotated duties from week to week, there being only a dozen or so families that participated in the small New Testament Baptist sect to which my parents had devoted themselves. The strict codes of behavior had been adapted from John R. Rice's publication *The Sword of the Lord* and from rigid lay interpretations of the Scripture that spoke to ecclesiastical rank and plain dress, the modesty of women, and separation from the world. The group had rented a Masonic Lodge in downtown Cleveland on the third floor of an imposing granite-fronted building, and every Sunday morning and evening and Wednesday night we climbed the flight of sixty-four stairs to the small auditorium with its elevated stage and electric organ, its bookshelves full of saints' lives, devotional guides, and Bible commentaries, its scarlet velvet draperies that gave our services an air of funereal solemnity.

"Gideon was a soldier of God," my father began the lesson. "He had the job of conquering the Midianites and the problem of how he was going to do it. The enemy army was so massive that the camel caravans that hauled their food and water stretched for miles. They had over 300,000 well-armed men. Gideon knew he was outnumbered, but God, who had already promised Gideon that his side would win, told him that he had too many soldiers. Too many? Gideon puzzled. Why, I have less than half the soldiers that the enemy does. You'll have to let the ones who are afraid

go home, said God. So Gideon obeyed and 10,000 men
were left. Now, said God, we will find out which of these
should fight."

My father got down on his knees in front of us. "Watch
the men drink, God told Gideon. The ones who lie down on
their bellies and lap water from the stream like dogs, send
home." My father, his tie tossed over his shoulder, lay down
on the wooden floor and showed us how they lapped. We
had never seen a Sunday-school teacher do such a thing. He
believed in what he was teaching and would do his best to
pass it on. "The ones who crouch down on one knee, drawing water to their mouths in a cupped hand, these are your
army." Gideon counted the soldiers posed like my father,
who, kneeling on one knee, was drinking water from his
hand: there were only three hundred men.

Now it was our turn to participate. We were the rem-
nant three hundred divided into three camps. My father,
who was Gideon, gave each of us an imaginary trumpet
and a pitcher with a torch in it. We surrounded the camp
of the Midianites, standing along the ridge of the valley of
Moreh, and when he gave the signal we broke open our
pitchers so the torches shone. With a blast on our horns we
shouted all together, *The sword of the Lord and of Gideon!*
In the valley below us that day we witnessed a great slaugh-
ter. Man turned on man in fear. Those who were not slain
fled. Our little group, led by my father, had tasted the des-
olation of the enemy and the sweet triumph of the people
who had sided with God.

What troubled me, despite Gideon's victory in the face
of overwhelming odds, was how to know whether to lap

water or to get down on your belly and slurp. These kinds of choices kept presenting themselves. God could choose you or as capriciously send you home. Or was there something about these soldiers that God could see and Gideon couldn't, for which the pose was a sign? "Look in my heart, God," I prayed. "You'll see."

My ideal of pure visibility may have had its origins in this story or another like it. It was less the lapping or the cupping that mattered, as I saw it, than a person's heart as only God could observe. And yet the church's and my parents' rules kept emphasizing a variety of outward acts. In order for God to see your inner life you had to keep polishing the surface. If a woman covered her head to show submission to her husband, if a man abstained from strong drink, if a young girl could refrain from dancing, if a boy did not take God's name in vain . . . these deeds were symptoms of the purified inner nature. We took each law literally, often taxing its spirit with our strivings. In every situation there was a right and a wrong behavioral response. I wanted my parents to see only good in me. I wanted to be good.

Stand in the light, I told myself, and sneaked off to meet my teacher in the English office on the second floor of the school. The light of God's eye from which nothing is hidden. The rest of me would have pleased them, except for the lies about where I'd been and the boyfriend I sported to seem innocent. Pretense—is that the unforgivable sin? They didn't have to know. I was in the uncompromised position, I told myself, of never having to lie on this point, because they never asked.

———

By the time I changed my name the first day of college, I had practiced enough shading of the truth to justify an adopted, if not wholly false, identity. "Day" was the current manifestation of Susan. Introducing myself, reflexively, I had the exhilarating rush of having fashioned a new being in the world, ex nihilo, that I could slip on and take off at will. She was not me, but I looked exactly like her. How long had I been waiting to call myself and have strangers call me by another name, so calling forth formerly inconceivable aspects of my personality? *Called to my Full—The Crescent dropped— / Existence's whole Arc, filled up, / With one small Diadem*, wrote Emily Dickinson. I had become easily memorable, my name a bright golden crown.

The new name and the new place, new friends who offered ways of seeing from another childhood's vantage, books, daily chapel, history—all this conspired to complicate my oversimple ideal of transparency. I was learning that the many aspects of identity, as it accumulated visages and appellations, social and spiritual vestments, the habits of inner lives, were not so easily aligned. The playing of roles had an ancient history: Cicero had written: "It is with perfect mental balance that I, one and single, sustain three roles—my own, that of my opponent, and that of our judge." We either tell the truth or conceal it, which I let myself believe was something other than lying.

By we I came to mean that insular three or more of us/me with somewhat less than perfect mental balance who loved, despised, and could adjudicate the strife. We sat outside in the early fall dusk and watched a moth, with barely a moth's power, drift, fluttering its wings, downward to the stones around the fountain. The wings like flower petals, rained on or ravaged by a predator, faltered as the moth landed. As quickly as its body touched solid ground, the wings had contracted into their prayer position—flat together, as thin as two scraps of paper. On the gray stone, the gray wings were camouflaged but true. What calms moths let it rest there, unflinching, as we watched. The moth was not the stone, but only we who had watched it land would know.

"Susan," Judson had startled me, "join me for dinner?" He had been so quiet. How long had he been standing there? He was the one person on campus who had refused to call me by my new name, and despite his refined good looks—his straight sandy hair always falling forward over his blue eyes—despite his love of beauty and his persistence with me, I didn't much like him at first. Who did he think I was?

"I'm not hungry, thanks," I lied.

In the trees beyond the pond a rustling startles me. A wind inside a wind, like an overheard interrogation. An army of questions, and I here by myself. I kneel down on one knee: where are my pitcher and torch?

You knew then that you were disappearing?

I couldn't tell him.

Do you think he noticed? You were so good at seeming one way and being another. You thought that if you had been in your mother's position you would have known.

Deep down it had to register. But he looked straight at me and didn't seem to notice anything missing, so for a while I thought it didn't matter. He never asked. I thought eventually I'd find my way back.

What if he wasn't there when you returned?

I kept wondering the same thing. You don't say to yourself, "Just a little farther . . ." It's progressive, but you don't notice that until you're almost gone.

Isn't a part of you true?

A part? It's an old animosity among selves that banishing the one costs all.

When I woke up this morning Judson said he was having a good dream about me. In gelid blue dreamlight, he was lying on the floor next to the bed and I was leaning over the edge, coming off the mattress onto him. "You were saying to me the way you do sometimes, 'This is not me, it is someone else.' " Yes, there are things about me I don't want to tell you. Such a good dream: one for all, all for one. Not that I might as well be anybody, or that you are actually the person I invent you as.

It's better that you don't know, that I look the other way. We are so little known as to slip away from our selves and the other one not notice. I am your wife. You will arrange my poems yet unpublished when I die. You will discover the pages that most alarm you in the drawer's deep culture, filed under someone else's name.

First let my elbows bear the weight of my torso, then ease that heaviness onto your chest, smothering your face in my hair. How far away could I be? How illicit? Close your eyes. The dream will happen before you know it.

What happens when the secret begins to keep you? You are no longer the one who fondles it, but when you sit it grasps you by the neck, when you rise it gnaws your heart raw with the dread of discovery. You are eating and sleeping less. You desperately need air. It is not guilt over my infidelity that grips me but the ongoing pretense I uphold of my trueheartedness.

I pretend I am a faithful wife. My husband is married to that faithful woman. The woman looks like me. She moves around in my body (this is what I mean, you can't tell by looking). He makes love to her. They talk in bed every night that he is not away on business before one or the other of them turns out the lights. He falls asleep happy. He says at a dinner party, "This has been the best year ever for our marriage." She excuses herself abruptly from the table, because to sit there would be to lie and she refuses to lie directly, unless she absolutely has to. He has asked her a question once or twice and she has heard herself reply with an avoidance.

"Is there anything you haven't told me? I want to know more of you, Susan." They spent last evening on opposite ends of the house, keeping things going, changing the music, refreshing people's drinks and trays of food.

"What makes you ask that tonight, after such a great party? All our friends here, scrumptious food. Didn't you enjoy yourself?" She unfastens her gold beaded bracelet and folds it carefully into its silk-lined box, replacing the lid.

"I saw the way Thom looked at you."

"There is absolutely nothing for you to worry about between me and anyone here tonight. Most definitely nothing's up with Thom." She concentrates on slowing down as she hangs up her belt and tosses her stockings in a basket of hand washing. "You're doing this jealous thing again. What kind of look?"

"Do you have any secrets from me?"

"A few." She will keep it light. "This is not my natural

hair color, quite, but the rest is real." She laughs and snaps
a towel at him, playfully. She hears their conversation from
the other side—she is he and he is she. She would ask what
else, but has momentarily distracted him from his chain of
disquiet. Or he has sensed a dark alley he's not ready to
skulk down. Didn't she drop a hint: not here, but elsewhere. Not tonight, but one eventful afternoon. "I've told
you everything you could possibly want to know, and more.
Do I bore you?"

He wraps his arms around her and she buries her face
in his neck. The smells of their friends and the children
blend on his clothes with the oils and heats of his concern.
Their clinging muffles the speed of their heartbeats. They
swallow their doubts.

In twelve years of marriage they have hit their walls
and have recovered, renewing vows, thriving after the initial
devastation of the mention of the two of them splitting.
Feelings between them deadened and, over time, unac-
countably, revived. The children have been a bond and their
own living through each other's virtual childhoods and
young adulthoods. They share an evolving faith that has
enlarged from parental imposition to a commitment of their
own to seek justice, to seek God. The thought of beginning
all over again, the view around them of friends launching
new marriages from the shoals of compromise and un-
healed hearts, the stress of divorce on friendships, let alone
the involved families, the savoring of pleasures they've en-
joyed knowing each other's beginnings and middle, and the
anticipation of growing older, possibly wiser, in each other's
company, how lucky they are and how hard they will work
to love—all this and her family's tumult conspire to keep
them trying.

I watch them. Where am I sitting? What persona is this that borrows that stagy semblance of my voice to cover for me? Now there are two of us, the invisible one and the artificial one. You cannot help despising someone satisfied with only part of you. They begin to blame themselves for why you don't love them. They grow weak with concern. You lie in the complete darkness. *I can do this*. The darkness comprehends you. How reassuring for something so entire, so extensive, to invite you in. The darker you go the less measurable, the less you need to answer the light's play over your parts. The more you disappear. Oblivion is easy to crave. So many of our poets do it: *The dead fly swept under the carpet, wrinkling to fulfillment.* "Give me that place where I'm erased." *Finally, this is what we craved,/ this lying in the bright light without distinction—*

Nothing done (even the language grows passive) matters: no name is on the act or on its perpetrator. Or else there are so many names no one will ever call Mister, Sappho, Family Man, Skipper, Man of My Dreams, Woman of God, ———, *Susan*. You are a mite on a dog's ear, you are a song sung in a thrush mouth, about nothing and for nothing, and against nothing, in the milk mouth of a sleeping child. The unconsoling notes play over and over, not repeating, but undoing, the whole outer gown of the body unraveling. No, wait!

One of those names is mine, no matter how far gone, isn't it? Are you listening? "Susan, are you up here?" I was in the room I write in, writing, and my husband, who had the dream and was listening to *Turandot* too loud for me to concentrate, came to the door of the room. He had found a photograph pressed between the pages of an old book.

Once again the appeal of cancellation—to disinherit one's birthright, to void all difference, entirely, to be indistinguishable, an even exchange between the vaporish blue and my breath—let go. That ancient artifact, my conscience, and it ached.

My mother is pulling on a white glove. It is a bright, cold Sunday morning, much like this one, and my father, sideways to the viewer, is buttoning my navy sailor coat for me. He is on one knee, smiling at his task. The tie he hasn't chosen hangs on the back of a cane seat chair. My hat cocks a little to one side across my bangs. I look over his shoulder straight into the camera.

"I'm heading out," Judson says. "Sure you don't want to come along?"

When he comes back I may not be here. I think of it more from his point of view, looking for me, than from mine, looking for another life. How could I imagine the distance from him I'd never intended to travel, the places I would go, or could go with a few hundred dollars. The separation.

I could picture him calling up the backstairs for me, wanting to tell me what everyone had said. Her car is in the driveway. He would look from the kitchen window out to the garden, where she might be spreading the winter's mulch. Not there. He would walk down the hill toward the pond, look in the shed, along the trail in the woods between our house and the neighbors'. He would call the neighbors, the phone ringing in their front hall, where he hopes she might be. Have you seen her?

But I am gone. Or I am on the far side of the pond and he finds me there and wants to talk.

Before you can confess the truth about yourself, the hurt of living incognito has to become a constant devastation. In every joy the tincture of regret, peacelessness, accusation. You must ache to love the one you've injured —whom you've injured out of contempt and need and incomprehension of the stakes—until you will die if you are not known. You must believe that if you can conceal the secret so well, he is certainly camouflaged from you. Your whole trust crumbles looking in at him, trust that you know him, that you could ever be known and loved in turn, trust in your own ability to see and, seeing, to love. This metamorphosis from contempt through apathy and back to love requires such perpetual devastation over time. It takes years to find the fetid, vengeful parts of infidelity and give those up. It takes more years to give up what felt like the healthy parts. It was there, on the outside of the marriage, that you practiced telling the truth.

You must understand that lying is a temporal invisibility. It's the leaves you wrap yourself in when the voice in the garden calls. I was learning to deflect any doubt or question about my faithfulness back onto the questioner, so that I didn't have to perpetuate the lie. I had for years part-lied, but mostly told the truth. Two and more irreconcilable parts. Which let me understand my father, or made me into him. There is a way to endure the self-split by numbing the parts, but I kept glimpsing the passion that the numbness depleted. I kept scrambling into the shadow of the numbness. What I could not do any longer was to conceive of myself as a person who said who I was out loud, the whole story, to anyone who thought it possible to love me.

Here was my father's ailment again, his dread of being known. There is a family with children on the line. I have another child in part to secure my recommitment to that anchor. What I really want is to be a worthy mother and wife. I force my family to serve as the same kind of false front I was raised to be for my father. Our presence testified to his normality. We failed, no matter how we strove for blessing, to discover the root of our calamity. I cannot shake his choice alone, I tell myself. So we slipped and fell, which is human, and he died stuck, and this gluey lie I keep perpetuating sticks to me like a curse revisited on the next generation. My father is in the window when I glance up, and in the hurried tone of my voice, in the shape of my ribs. What if, lights on, as is, he had asked us to love him?

This is the common wisdom: Tell what you can bear to tell. Tell what you think the person you have wronged can bear. Don't tell to punish. Don't tell to relieve yourself of the load of your own guilt. To tell her will destroy her. To tell him will ruin everything he has lived for. Wait for the right time for them, which may never come. Wait until they ask, point-blank, and then decide if you are ready. Are the consequences worth it? Sometimes they are. Sometimes they aren't. Write it down before you say it. Say it before you chicken out. There is a man I know who could forgive. There is a woman I know who would kill herself to spite you.

For five years I weighed the common wisdom daily. I knew men who had been discovered "cheating" and whose long-suffering wives took on the hurt as their own deficiency. I have a woman friend who told the truth and whose husband took their children from her. He spent years and

fortunes battling in court to prove her betrayal's unforgiv-
ability, meanwhile fathering a second family with their babysitter; now they all sit side by side on bleachers at baseball
games, their lives entangled and halved.

I opened the book I had slipped into my jacket pocket
and read:

> *Lord, who shall abide in thy tabernacle?*
> *who shall dwell in thy holy hill?*
> *He that walketh uprightly, and worketh righteousness,*
> *and speaketh the truth in his heart.*
>
> *Who shall ascend into the hill of the Lord?*
> *or who shall stand in his holy place?*
> *He that hath clean hands and a pure heart;*
> *who hath not lifted up his soul unto vanity,*
> *nor sworn deceitfully.*

If her hands are clean and her heart pure—I had been
forgiven. But I had yet to go to the man I had wronged (and
whom I desperately wanted to love me) to cancel my ongoing lie, my maintaining the family pattern of dishonesty.

My husband couldn't bear ever to look at me again.
Hadn't my family put him through enough already? Wasn't
I a hard pill he had to swallow and swallow? He would
remarry within the year, a woman of fidelity and beauty
and a way with children, my children. What kind of stories
would they be told about me? All that we had made
together—I took inventory—did not add up to the ultimate
banishment of the untruthful from the presence of God.

"If you give me the opportunity, Lord, one more time,

whatever the consequence," I prayed, "I will tell the truth."
And then I asked God for the power to make a choice my
father must have wished he could, the choice to live free
of the lie. *That we henceforth be no more children, tossed to
and fro, and carried about with every wind of doctrine, by
the sleight of men, and cunning craftiness, whereby they lie
in wait to deceive; but speaking the truth in love, may grow
up into Him in all things, which is the head, even Christ.*

Judson put the question simply, the same one as before.
I hadn't gone away, but had sat in the sun and read and
drunk my coffee uninterrupted. (Maybe it was a morning
unlike any my father had ever been given.) When he came
home later that morning is when he asked.

"Is there something you would like to tell me?" There
was a reason my husband was unable to retire his doubts.
I had made an offer of honesty, yes, but hadn't thought the
test would come so soon. Walking out on the plank of my
own promise, I peered down at the water. First you leave
your father's house and then your own. There was a deep
gulf below me I could not see into. This was the last of my
life as I knew it. "Whatever the consequence," I said inside
my head to remind myself, breathing once. He could tell
in the stillness of the pause between his question and my
looking back up at him that his life was changing too.